University of Michigan Business School Management Series

INNOVATIVE SOLUTIONS TO THE PRESSING PROBLEMS OF BUSINESS

The mission of the University of Michigan Business School Management Series is to provide accessible, practical, and cutting-edge solutions to the most critical challenges facing businesspeople today. The UMBS Management Series provides concepts and tools for people who seek to make a significant difference in their organizations. Drawing on the research and experience of faculty at the University of Michigan Business School, the books are written to stretch thinking while providing practical, focused, and innovative solutions to the pressing problems of business.

Also available in the UMBS series:

Becoming a Better Value Creator, by Anjan V. Thakor

Achieving Success Through Social Capital, by Wayne Baker

Improving Customer Satisfaction, Loyalty, and Profit,
by Michael D. Johnson and Anders Gustafsson

The Compensation Solution, by John E. Tropman

Strategic Interviewing, by Richaurd Camp, Mary Vielhaber,
and Jack L. Simonetti

Creating the Multicultural Organization, by Taylor Cox

Getting Results, by Clinton O. Longenecker and
Jack L. Simonetti

A Company of Leaders, by Gretchen M. Spreitzer and
Robert E. Quinn

Managing the Unexpected, by Karl Weick and Kathleen Sutcliffe

Using the Law for Competitive Advantage, by George J. Siedel

Creativity at Work, by Jeff DeGraff and Katherine A. Lawrence

Making I/T Work, by Dennis G. Severance and Jacque Passino

Decision Management, by J. Frank Yates

For additional information on any of these titles or future
titles in the series, visit www.umbsbooks.com.

Executive Summary

This book will help managers make day-to-day decisions on how best to manage their employees while also protecting their companies and themselves from legal liability. Most managers in executive education programs are surprised at the breadth of discretion the law often gives them. They also tend to be surprised, though, at some of the subtle and unnecessary mistakes managers make that cause legal headaches for themselves and for their companies. Becoming familiar with basic principles of employment law will enable managers to develop an internal compass on workforce issues.

Unlike most employment law books for managers, which contain lists of laws and an abundance of legalese, this book is organized around the types of issues managers face in the workplace:

- Understanding the basic principles of U.S. employment law and how it compares with other countries (Chapter One)
- Hiring and promoting employees (Chapter Two)
- Evaluating your current employees, checking the work history of applicants, and providing references for former employees (Chapter Three)
- Avoiding illegal discrimination in your workforce and minimizing liability if discrimination does occur (Chapter Four)

- Managing employees with disabilities and issues of lost work time (Chapter Five)
- Terminating employees (Chapter Six)

Each chapter focuses on legal concepts of broad application in today's workplace, providing real examples of problems faced by managers and explaining strategies for managers dealing with similar issues. Each chapter contains "Fact or Fallacy?" boxes that prompt readers to test their understanding of legal principles. The ensuing discussion explains why each item is a fact or a fallacy. This book does not, however, give specific legal advice or eliminate the need for managers to seek advice from human resources professionals and employment law attorneys. Instead, it helps managers develop a toolkit for assessing the need to seek advice and for working with advisers to achieve the best result for the company.

In short, this book gives managers practical information on how to minimize legal problems when hiring, promoting, supervising, evaluating, and terminating employees. It also shows how the legal principles frequently help managers reach workforce decisions that are carefully considered and fundamentally fair, *and* that reflect good management practices. Managers can use the strategies and information in this book to select, motivate, and lead their employees with greater confidence and effectiveness.

A Manager's Guide to Employment Law

How to Protect Your Company and Yourself

Dana M. Muir

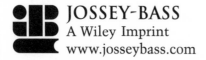

JOSSEY-BASS
A Wiley Imprint
www.josseybass.com

Published by Jossey-Bass
A Wiley Imprint
989 Market Street, San Francisco, CA 94103-1741   www.josseybass.com

Jossey-Bass books and products are available through most bookstores. To contact
Jossey-Bass directly call our Customer Care Department within the U.S. at (800) 956-7739,
outside the U.S. at (317) 572-3986 or fax (317) 572-4002.

Jossey-Bass also publishes its books in a variety of electronic formats. Some content
that appears in print may not be available in electronic books.

Library of Congress Cataloging-in-Publication Data

Muir, Dana M., date.
  A manager's guide to employment law: how to protect your company and
yourself/Dana M. Muir.—1st ed.
      p. cm.—(The University of Michigan Business School management
series)
Includes bibliographical references and index.
  ISBN 0-7879-6404-2 (alk. paper)
  1. Labor laws and legislation—United States. 2. Labor
contract—United States. 3. Executives—United States—Handbooks,
manuals, etc. I. Title. II. Series.
  KF3455.Z9M85   2003
  344.7301—dc21

                                                      2003001774

Printed in the United States of America
FIRST EDITION
HB Printing   10 9 8 7 6 5 4 3 2 1

Contents

Series Foreword

Welcome to the University of Michigan Business School Management Series. The books in this series address the most urgent problems facing business today. The series is part of a larger initiative at the University of Michigan Business School (UMBS) that ties together a range of efforts to create and share knowledge through conferences, survey research, interactive and distance training, print publications, and news media.

It is just this type of broad-based initiative that sparked my love affair with UMBS in 1984. From the day I arrived I was enamored with the quality of the research, the quality of the MBA program, and the quality of the Executive Education Center. Here was a business school committed to new lines of research, new ways of teaching, and the practical application of ideas. It was a place where innovative thinking could result in tangible outcomes.

The UMBS Management Series is one very important outcome, and it has an interesting history. It turns out that every year five thousand participants in our executive program fill out a marketing survey in which they write statements indicating the most important problems they face. One day Lucy Chin, one of our administrators, handed me a document containing all these statements. A content analysis of the data resulted in a list of forty-five pressing problems. The topics ranged from growing a company to managing personal stress. The list covered a wide territory, and I started to see its potential. People in organizations tend to be driven by a very traditional set of problems, but the solutions evolve. I went to my friends at Jossey-Bass to discuss a publishing project. The discussion eventually grew into the University of Michigan Business School Management Series— Innovative Solutions to the Pressing Problems of Business.

The books are independent of each other, but collectively they create a comprehensive set of management tools that cut across all the functional areas of business—from strategy to human resources to finance, accounting, and operations. They draw on the interdisciplinary research of the Michigan faculty. Yet each book is written so a serious manager can read it quickly and act immediately. I think you will find that they are books that will make a significant difference to you and your organization.

Robert E. Quinn, Consulting Editor
M.E. Tracy Distinguished Professor
University of Michigan Business School

Preface

M anagers are constantly challenged in today's business environment to do more with fewer employees, to motivate diverse groups of employees, and to face up to tough people problems in their workforce. One key to your success is accomplishing those goals while protecting yourself and your company from legal liability. Human resources departments, management consultants, and even lawyers all claim to help managers select, motivate, and winnow out their employees. I have spent most of the last twenty-five years in those roles—as a human resources executive, as a practicing lawyer, and as a leader of management education sessions.

I often find that managers are frustrated with the legal system. Their interactions with human resources professionals, management consultants, and attorneys have convinced them that those people are more likely to put roadblocks in the way of progress than to help managers solve problems. Managers tend to blame legal requirements for the roadblocks. U.S. law, however, provides managers with broad discretion in many employment-related situations. In fact, in most instances, the law helps ensure that managers perform their essential functions in a way that is fundamentally fair and that respects important societal values while still supporting the managers' goal of meeting the challenges of the current business environment.

I have written this book to correct many of the fallacies about employment law that have become ingrained in managers' beliefs and to help managers confront the people problems they face with their employees. Employment law books tend to be organized according to the many laws that govern workplace decisions. In my experience, though, most managers do not want or need lengthy technical discussions of the myriad of federal and state employment laws. If you have an employee who misses a great deal of work due to illness, you usually do not want to read a chapter on the Americans With Disabilities Act, another chapter on the Family Medical Leave Act, and yet another chapter on Workers' Compensation. Worse yet, in books organized on those principles you are left figuring out which of the laws applies to your situation and how those laws might fit together. Then, finally, you are left to seek the details relevant to the resolution of your problem. Instead of all the legalese, most managers with that type of problem want to know the basic concepts that govern absence from work and how the concepts interrelate. Given that information, managers have the basis of knowledge to make decisions or seek additional advice.

This book departs from other employment law books by being organized around topics of interest to managers. This enables you to identify the type of workplace problem you are interested in and to go to the correct chapter for practical insights and examples. Here I have taken the usual employment legal issues and organized them according to the following challenges faced by managers:

- Chapter Two: How to select the best employee for a job, whether you are promoting from within or hiring from outside the company.

- Chapter Three: How to avoid current and future employment law issues when doing performance evaluations of existing employees and when providing references for former employees.
- Chapter Four: How to avoid situations of discrimination and harassment in the workplace and what to do if complaints occur. This is the most general chapter in the book, and the same concepts come up in hiring, evaluating, disciplining, and firing employees.
- Chapter Five: How to deal with disabled employees and employees who miss excessive amounts of work. This is the most complex chapter in the book and includes a variety of examples to illustrate how the laws interact.
- Chapter Six: How to terminate employees for poor performance, in times of downsizing, and in reorganizations.

These chapters provide managers with the tools to consider the legal implications of their workplace decisions. Chapter One lays the groundwork by providing a general overview of the U.S. legal system as it relates to employment. Nonetheless, what this book does not do is substitute for the three years of law school, the years of legal practice, and the detailed research in your state that enable good employment law attorneys to address legal questions specifically and in depth. Nor does this book provide specific legal advice about actual situations you will encounter. Finally, it makes no attempt to cover the myriad of state-specific laws that govern the workplace. Instead, I intend the book to add a basic understanding of employment law concepts to your managerial toolkit. My goal is to help you establish an internal compass to assist you in making day-to-day decisions in real time. You will also be better able to apply the advice you receive from human resources professionals, management consultants, and lawyers. You should be confident in your ability to engage those advisers in conversation, and you

should be better able to determine when you need to seek professional legal advice and counsel.

■ Acknowledgments

I have many people to thank for their help with this book. First and foremost, Jack Simonetti welcomed me into the Basic Management executive education course that he has taught here at the University of Michigan Business School for more than two decades. My experience with the many business managers who have passed through that course in recent years serves as the foundation for this book. Jack is a master at helping business managers reach their potential, has been a marvelous mentor to me, and never stopped pestering me—in a positive way—about when this book would be complete.

Bob Quinn, who conceived the series, provided important ideas for the development of this book's focus. My colleagues George Cameron, Cindy Schipani, and George Siedel have given me numerous opportunities over the past ten years to pursue my interest in employment law, served as sounding boards, and supported my work on this book. I appreciate the careful reviews done by Susan Call and Terry Dworkin. John Bergez provided invaluable encouragement and editorial assistance with good humor, a manager's eye for what would be important to my readers, and infinite patience.

Finally, this title would not exist without the input and support of my brother, Darryl Muir, but I still am not giving him any share in the royalties!

February 2003   Dana M. Muir
Ann Arbor, Michigan

Employment Law from a Manager's Perspective

P ut yourself in the shoes of Wendy's employer. When Wendy caught her husband looking at an adult Internet site, she convinced him that it would spice up their marriage if they set up a similar site. Wendy posed for provocative photographs, which her husband took and posted to their site. To access the site, a viewer had to claim to be an adult. Professionally, Wendy worked as a counselor to troubled youths. One of the youth's parents told Wendy's manager about the Web site and demanded that Wendy be fired.

As Wendy's manager, what would you do? More important, what factors would you consider in making your decision? Would it matter if Wendy had a long history of excellent performance appraisals? What if Wendy had done all the work for the Web site on her own time and with her own computer equipment?

Certainly, one of the factors in your thinking would need to be potential legal issues. As a manager, you don't want to cause your company or yourself unnecessary legal complications, such as lawsuits for wrongful termination. More positively, you need to know what latitude the law does and does not give you in your efforts to build and manage the best possible workforce.

All too often I have seen managers who are frustrated with the legal system. After frequent interactions with human resources professionals, management consultants, and attorneys, managers end up believing that the law requires them to hire a certain job candidate even though another candidate is far more qualified, that they cannot discipline the employee who spends more time out of work because of illness than at work, or that the law prevents them from firing an employee whose performance is lousy. All of these beliefs are fallacies. With a proper understanding of the law, managers can hire the most qualified workers. Managers can discipline employees for unreasonable absences. And managers can fire employees who cannot or will not perform the critical functions of their jobs.

As a manager, you can always get specific legal advice for some issue that confronts you, and often you should. On the other hand, you don't want to run up the cost, whether in time or money, of seeking professional counsel every time an employment question arises that might have legal implications. To manage efficiently, you need an internal compass that can guide much of your everyday decision making and let you know when you really need to get expert advice. Developing that internal compass is the purpose of this book.

This first chapter provides the basic road map for considering the legal implications of almost any employment-related decision you might make. In the pages that follow, I first explain the primary concept underlying U.S. employment law, *employment-at-will.* Next I summarize some key exceptions to the basic rule. To provide some perspective, I then briefly compare the U.S. system and the approach taken by many other developed countries.

The discussion of employment-at-will shows that as a manager you have significant flexibility in dealing with workforce issues in the United States. However, the nature of our legal system has some implications that can be at least as important as the substantive legal rules when you are evaluating a potential employment decision. Therefore, I also address some unique features of the U.S. legal system.

Finally, it's important to understand that managing legal risk and opportunity in employment decisions is just a special case of what you already do as a manager. Accordingly, I end the chapter by integrating the discussion of U.S. employment law with the basic concepts of managerial risk taking.

■ Employment-at-Will

The underlying concept governing the legal relationship between employer and employee in the United States is known as *employment-at-will.* The concept itself is surprisingly simple to understand. It becomes complex only because of the exceptions that have developed over time. Before reading on, though, try your hand at the following Fact or Fallacy? questions.

■ Fact or Fallacy? ■		
1. You don't need good cause to legally fire an employee.	□ Fact	□ Fallacy
2. Unless you put a promise to an employee in writing, the promise will not be enforceable.	□ Fact	□ Fallacy

■ **Fact or Fallacy?, Cont'd** ■

3. You cannot make any decisions about an
   employee or potential employee based on the
   person's physical characteristics.   ☐ Fact   ☐ Fallacy

4. You can make decisions on who to send to
   training based on employees' gender because
   nondiscrimination laws do not apply to decisions
   such as training.   ☐ Fact   ☐ Fallacy

5. You would have more flexibility in firing employees
   if you managed a workforce in almost any
   developed economy other than the United States. ☐ Fact   ☐ Fallacy

The Basic Rule

At its most basic, the principle of employment-at-will permits
you, as a manager, to fire an employee for any reason, whether
it is a good reason, a bad reason, or even no reason at all, so long
as any reason that you do have is not an *illegal* reason. Historically, the logic behind this rule was that employees and employers should both enjoy roughly the same amount of freedom
in establishing the terms of their relationship. Since employees
generally were free to change jobs at will, employers also had
the right to terminate the employment relationship at will. Individuals typically are employees at will when they are hired
without a contract that specifies the duration of the employment
or that imposes other obligations on the employer.

The employment-at-will standard also recognizes that companies are in the best position to determine their own employment needs. The law acknowledges that you need flexibility in
determining the size of your workforce and the skills you require
to get the job done. As a result, it shouldn't surprise you that
courts have upheld the right of managers to fire employees for
poor performance, for misrepresenting their credentials, and for
insubordination. It may come as more of a surprise that courts

have permitted managers to fire employees for being suspected of having an affair with the boss's son or because the employee's spouse, a police officer, ticketed the manager's wife. Whatever the merits of these reasons, none of them is specifically prohibited by law.

The first Fact or Fallacy? item is therefore true. As a manager, you may fire an employee for any reason, even a lousy, arbitrary, or unfair reason, so long as it is not an illegal reason. Practically speaking, though, few managers choose to fire employees for lousy, arbitrary, or unfair reasons. Managers who act so arbitrarily not only sometimes fire good employees, they also contribute to poor morale and can make it difficult to attract skilled workers. In addition, it is legitimate to ask whether judges and juries look askance at managers who appear to have treated a good employee unfairly. So the advice here is not that you should start treating your employees arbitrarily or fire them for writing with blue instead of black pens. But it is useful to understand that the foundational concept of U.S. employment law recognizes your rights as a manager, within the constraints believed by our society to be appropriate, to make decisions about your employees' employment.

Consider how the employment-at-will standard would apply to Wendy. The beginning premise is that you, as Wendy's manager, have the right to fire her at will, so long as your reason is not illegal. Consequently, you can begin with the premise that you may fire her for working with her husband to establish the Web site and for permitting provocative pictures of herself to appear on the site. The only remaining question is whether any exception exists that would make your reason for firing Wendy illegal.

Exceptions to the Basic Rule

If applied without limitation, the concept of employment-at-will would permit a manager to fire an employee at any time for any reason. But the courts and legislatures have developed limitations to prevent managers from making employment decisions based on criteria that our society defines as unacceptable, such as certain types of discrimination.

These limitations, which act as exceptions to the concept of employment-at-will, sometimes frustrate managers because they are not always well defined. Still, you can get a grasp of the main limitations by understanding three basic categories of exceptions to employment-at-will: contracts, nondiscrimination statutes, and policy-based and statutory provisions.

Contractual Exceptions

Some of the contractual exceptions to employment-at-will are obvious. When an employer enters into a written contract to employ an individual for a specific time period and with specific terms, that contract typically is enforceable. For example, top executives, coaches of professional sports teams, and actors in television sitcoms frequently have written contracts of this type. In contrast to those individualized contracts, a written collective bargaining agreement typically covers groups of employees in a unionized workplace. I devote little coverage in this book to the specialized issues of dealing with unionized employees because less than 10 percent of nongovernmental workers in the United States are unionized. If you do manage unionized employees, though, you should recognize that properly negotiated collective bargaining agreements are enforceable contracts. In addition, in a unionized workplace a separate and distinct set of federal laws governs employee—management relations.

More subtle issues of a contractual nature arise when a manager makes a verbal promise to an employee or to a recruit. Those promises might be enforceable if they are clear enough that the terms of the promise can be understood and a reasonable person would think the manager had the authority to make such a promise. Another factor that might affect the legal analysis is whether the employee or job candidate relied on the verbal promise in taking some action, such as quitting an existing job or turning down another job offer.

Consider what happened to Philip McConkey, who went to work for Ross & Co. as an insurance broker after playing football for the New York Giants. Alexander & Alexander (A&A) made considerable efforts to recruit McConkey, even arranging a meeting between its CEO and McConkey. At the meeting the CEO addressed McConkey's worry that A&A was up for sale and "assured him there was no intention to sell."[1] The company's chairman allegedly gave McConkey similar assurances. McConkey eventually accepted a position with A&A, but the company was sold later the same year. Less than a year after employing him, the company stripped McConkey of all responsibilities and subsequently laid him off. When McConkey learned that A&A had been negotiating the sale of the company at the same time it was recruiting him, he sued. A jury awarded him more than $10 million.

Fact or Fallacy? item 2 is therefore a fallacy. In practice, it can be difficult for judges and juries to evaluate who is telling the truth when employees and managers tell different stories about verbal promises allegedly made to employees or recruits. Nevertheless, verbal commitments can be enforceable. Moreover, casual written assurances can be as legally binding as a long, formal document that has been evaluated by the company's lawyers. As a manager, you should be circumspect about the commitments you make to your employees, whether or not you put them in writing.

Not all verbal representations are enforceable, however. Giles Wanamaker, in-house counsel for a company, alleged that he was told by a vice president and director that the job was a "career" job. Others reportedly told him "that there was no need for concern in that the position would be a job for the balance of [his] career."[2] After he was fired, Giles sued for breach of contract. He lost because New York law requires that oral promises must be very clear in establishing a fixed period for employment; otherwise the basic rule of employment-at-will governs.

Many companies have taken steps to ensure that their employees understand that they are at-will employees. Offer letters, employment manuals, and other official company communications often explicitly explain employment-at-will. In addition, a company can take two steps to reduce the chances that its managers will make promises that undercut its employment-at-will relationships. First, the company can train its managers so they understand that careless statements might become enforceable commitments. In a column on how to retain valuable employees during times of economic retrenchment, the *Wall Street Journal* recently advised, "Bosses should 'whisper in the ears of those who keep their companies afloat that they're wanted—and will be rewarded with salary increases and bonuses.'"[3] That is a fine tactic—so long as the bosses and their companies understand that those whispers may be legally enforceable contracts. As a second tactic, the company can include language in its statements of at-will status explaining that only very specific agreements can change that status. In its offer letters to new hires, one major high-tech company first states that the person will be an at-will employee and explains what that means. Then it includes language similar to the following: "Your status as an at-will employee can be modified only by an explicit written agreement signed by both you and [the name of the company president]." This helps to ensure that a manager cannot undercut the company's at-will policy in recruiting a new employee or trying to retain a current one. In the long run, that protection is good for the company and its managers.

The application of the implied contract exception to employment-at-will is fairly easy in Wendy's case. Typically, in evaluating the potential existence of an implied contract, you would consider a variety of possibilities, such as an individualized written contract with Wendy, an employee handbook that indicates the company will terminate employees only for good cause or that establishes a defined disciplinary procedure, or the existence of other verbal or written commitments. Since there is no indication in the facts that as Wendy's employer you have limited your ability to fire her, it appears that Wendy is an at-will employee and the implied contract exception will not limit your alternatives.

Nondiscrimination Statutory Exceptions

Perhaps the best known but least understood limitations on a manager's right to fire employees are those based in nondiscrimination law. Chapter Four discusses in some detail how to avoid discrimination and harassment in the workplace. Because of the importance of these concepts in the basic analysis of any workforce decision, though, I include a brief primer here.

Federal law prohibits an employer from discriminating against an employee or job candidate based on race, color, gender, national origin, religion, pregnancy, age of forty or older, and disability. State nondiscrimination laws generally are similar to the federal laws, but many protect additional characteristics of employees and job applicants. For example, several states and over a hundred cities and counties have laws that protect against discrimination on the basis of sexual orientation. Michigan protects people against differential treatment based on height and weight. Alaska forbids employers from acting on the basis of a change in marital status, and North Dakota does not permit receipt of public assistance to be a factor in employment-related decisions. Even localities sometimes impose specific prohibitions against discrimination in employment.

As stated, then, Fact or Fallacy? item 3 is mostly fact, but it is difficult to evaluate because it is so inclusive. As you will see in Chapter Five, federal nondiscrimination law makes it illegal to discriminate against someone with a disability who, with or without reasonable accommodation, can perform the essential functions of a job. That, on its own, means that the law restricts what physical characteristics you can consider when making employment-related decisions. Similarly, some state laws, such as Michigan's protection of height and weight, further restrict your ability to make determinations based on physical characteristics. More subtle legal problems also can arise from issues associated with physical characteristics. More and more employees or former employees are filing lawsuits claiming their employer discriminated against them because of their appearance. For example, a court permitted a former employee to sue a ski resort that fired the individual for not having any upper teeth and refusing to wear her dentures, which she said caused her pain. The resort said it was concerned with its public image and had a policy that "employees will be expected to have teeth and to wear them daily to work."[4] In the view of the court, however, the toothless chambermaid's claim could fall within the ambit of the law against disability discrimination.

The extent to which you may consider physical characteristics depends primarily on two variables. The first is the law of the relevant state. Second, the job may require a specific physical characteristic. For example, it could be impossible for someone who is very tall to perform a job in a confined space that cannot be expanded.

The prohibition on discrimination tends to cover all phases of employment, such as salary, benefits, access to training, promotion, and all other terms, conditions, or privileges of employment. Consequently, Fact or Fallacy? item 4 is a fallacy. The federal laws against discrimination protect employees against a wide variety of discriminatory acts in the workplace, including any acts that affect the employee's "terms, conditions, and privileges" of employment. Access to training, which can qualify an employee for a promotion, raise, or even continued employment, certainly is a privilege of employment.

During recent years, one of the most quickly growing categories of employment lawsuits has been suits alleging retaliation for making a complaint of discrimination. Between 1992 and 2000 the number of retaliation lawsuits almost doubled. In addition to the raw numbers, there is some evidence that juries are particularly hostile to employers who retaliate against employees who complain of discrimination. For example, a manager in Iowa who claimed that her employer retaliated against her because she complained of gender discrimination won more than $80 million in a jury award.[5]

One concern with application of the nondiscrimination laws occurs because of the "he said–she said" nature of the claims that arise. If you fire Wendy because you believe that her involvement in the Web site undermines her ability to do her job, or even because you simply disapprove of her actions, then it does not appear you have violated any federal, state, or local nondiscrimination laws. No jurisdiction that I know of specifically protects individuals who establish and appear in provocative Web sites from being discriminated against on that basis. Suppose, however, that Wendy claims that the reason you have given for her firing is a pretext and that the real reason was that she is a woman. Given the number of cases in which the employee argues that the employer had a prohibited discriminatory reason for a particular action, even while stating a different reason entirely, the law has developed a specific approach for evaluating these contradictory claims. Chapter Four discusses that approach. But for now, consider whether Wendy has a stronger case if male employees have been permitted to establish and appear on similar Web sites. Or what if the employer has a pattern of firing women, but not men, for engaging in unsavory behavior outside the workplace? In such cases, the disparity of treatment may increase the likelihood that a judge or jury will find that the employer discriminated against Wendy because of her gender. I'll return to this issue in Chapter Four.

Policy-Based and Statutory Exceptions in Your Jurisdiction
The most unpredictable category of exceptions to the principle
of employment-at-will is made up of policy-based exceptions established by the courts and miscellaneous statutory exceptions
in various jurisdictions. Even here, however, there are some
trends that are of general interest to managers.

The first trend concerns public policy exceptions to the
basic at-will principle. An employer might find itself embroiled
in a wrongful termination lawsuit when it fires an employee for
a reason that on the surface does not violate any state law, but
that in some way undercuts the policies being protected by state
law. One recurring fact pattern involves employers who fire employees for refusing to do something illegal. A trucker might refuse to drive an overweight load. An inspector in a food
processing plant might refuse to approve a product that does
not meet minimum safety standards. A worker at a nuclear
power plant might refuse to falsify operating documents. Perhaps not surprisingly, workers tend to win these types of cases.
Courts reason that an employee should not be forced to choose
between keeping a job and complying with the law. Furthermore, because public policy exceptions tend to be tort claims,
they provide the opportunity for plaintiffs to receive high damage awards. Therefore, aside from the ethical implications, no
manager should ever ask an employee to do something that is
illegal.

But when the facts are different, many jurisdictions con-
strue the public policy exception quite narrowly. In one recent
case Karen Bammert worked for Don Williams, who owned
Don's SuperValu. Karen's husband, a police officer, arrested
Don's wife for driving under the influence of alcohol. Don fired
Karen in retaliation for the arrest. Karen then sued, alleging that
her firing violated Wisconsin public policy because her husband
had an affirmative legal obligation to assist in the arrest of Don's
wife and because state policy discouraged drunken driving. The

Wisconsin Supreme Court decided that it would be pushing public policy too far to consider the legal duties of an employee's spouse. So, the basic policy of employment-at-will applied, and Karen lost the case.[6]

A somewhat similar concept is known as the good faith and fair dealing exception. Courts interpret most contracts, such as a contract for the sale of goods, to require the parties to deal with one another fairly and in good faith, even if the contract does not explicitly address this point. Employees have argued that employers owe the same duty to their employees because even an at-will employment relationship is based on contract law principles. If generally accepted, this exception would substantially corrode the rule of employment-at-will. Remember, historically you could fire employees for an arbitrary reason, such as writing with a blue pen instead of a black one. But if the law requires you to deal fairly and in good faith with your employees, at minimum it seems you would have to give the blue pen users a warning before you fired them.

It makes sense, then, that only a relatively small number of employees have won cases based on an implied duty of good faith and fair dealing. If an employer takes an egregious action, such as firing a star employee the day before payment of a sales bonus in order to avoid paying the bonus, then the employee may have a reasonable chance of winning on this theory. However, one recent case decided by the California Supreme Court emphasized how infrequently this exception applies. Over twenty-two years of employment, John Guz had successfully worked his way up the ranks in Bechtel National Inc. When Bechtel eliminated a division, it fired Guz. He argued that Bechtel's restructuring decisions and his firing were arbitrary. Guz lost when the court determined that, as an at-will employee, he was only entitled to the benefit of promises made by his employer, and Bechtel had never promised him continuing employment.[7] Because California often sets employment law trends, it appears that the implied duty of good faith and fair dealing will not be important in most employment law cases.

Another category of exceptions to the doctrine of employment-at-will exists because states and other jurisdictions sometimes choose to protect employees from specific actions that might be taken by employers. These are probably the most varied exceptions and tend to be limited in theory only by the imagination of state lawmakers, and in practice by the desire of most states to encourage employment in the state. A few examples provide a sense of the scope of these exceptions. Numerous states provide protection to whistle-blowers, people who serve as jurors, and even employees who engage in specified conduct on their own time. Indiana has a "Smoker's Rights Law" that precludes employers from firing employees for using tobacco outside the workplace.

New York goes further in its protection of employees outside the workplace and prohibits employers from firing someone for engaging in legal activities, including "recreational activities." That law has led to some interesting cases. For example, Wal-Mart had a nonfraternization policy that prohibited a "dating relationship" between a married employee and any employee other than the spouse. The company fired both Laurel, who was separated from her husband, and Samuel because the two were dating. The state sued to have the employees reinstated, arguing that the employees' right to date qualified for protection under the law protecting recreational activities. On appeal, a New York court decided in Wal-Mart's favor. According to the judges, "'dating' is entirely distinct from and, in fact, bears little resemblance to 'recreational activity.'"[8] Therefore, the basic employment-at-will standard applied, and Wal-Mart could legally fire the employees for dating. This type of interpretative question, however, is a difficult one for the courts and other courts using the same statute have held differently.

Consider now whether any of these exceptions would protect Wendy. You have not ordered her to do anything illegal. Nor does it seem likely that any state has a strong public policy in favor of titillating Web sites. So Wendy is unlikely to have a valid claim based on a generalized public policy exception. Nor is your act in firing her the egregious kind of act that tends to run afoul of the good faith and fair dealing exception. You should, though, check to see whether your state protects employees against being fired for engaging in activities outside the workplace. It is possible that a state law covering a broad range of endeavors, such as recreational activities, would affect your decision to fire Wendy. Those laws are so new, and the situation is so unique, that the legal analysis may not be entirely clear. At the end of the chapter I will return to the topic of evaluating and managing these types of risk.

■ International Comparisons

Employment law in the United States has developed a reputation for preventing managers from firing lousy employees, so much so that many managers, both here and abroad, subscribe to Fact or Fallacy? item 5. By now though, you know that you actually have considerable flexibility in making employment decisions. For additional perspective on this issue, it is worth comparing U.S. law to the law of other developed countries. To put this comparison in context, consider two separate situations.

First, you are a manager at a large company that has been affected by a slowing economy. You need to downsize. Would you rather be located in the United States or in Western Europe?

In the United States, the basic rules are the ones outlined so far in this chapter and the Worker Adjustment and Retraining Act (WARN). WARN requires large businesses to provide employees and the state with sixty days' written notice when laying off groups of employees. Otherwise, you may set any criteria you choose and lay off as many employees as you choose, so long as you do not use any illegal criteria.

In many other countries with developed economies, the law is more stringent and might significantly limit your options. Other countries would still permit you to fire an employee for cause, such as for stealing from the company. But in other situations, such as downsizing, employees are entitled to notice and compensation. The amount owed to an employee usually depends on the individual's length of employment. In Germany that might mean up to seven months' notice or pay, if a layoff can be negotiated at all. And in Germany, in deciding which workers to lay off you must choose those who will be least socially affected by the layoff. That means that older workers, disabled workers, and workers with families receive the most protection.

Second, imagine you have a key employee who has become pregnant. In the United States, the Pregnancy Discrimination Act requires you to treat pregnant women equivalently to other employees. They are therefore entitled to be covered by your regular sick leave policy. If you do not provide paid sick leave for other illnesses, then federal law does not require you to pay the pregnant employee for the time she is off work due to illness associated with the pregnancy or delivery of her child. In addition, the Family and Medical Leave Act (FMLA) guarantees up to twelve weeks of unpaid leave and typically requires you return the person to her job at the end of her leave. Even then, though, the FMLA excludes from its protections certain key employees.

Compare Hong Kong and Switzerland. In each of those countries, employers must provide eight weeks of full pay for maternity leave. In France women are entitled to up to twenty-six weeks off work, with salary substitution paid by government programs. In Australia women are entitled to a full year of maternity leave.

In short, workers in other industrialized countries often receive more protection than U.S. law provides. France has a thirty-five-hour maximum work week. Employees there receive a minimum of five weeks vacation a year and eleven paid holidays. Volkswagen in Germany has a 29.9-hour work week. Unionization rates in Western Europe are higher than in the United States, and generous government-sponsored pension programs have supported retirement at relatively early ages. The European Union (EU) is also developing directives that ban discrimination based on age and sexual orientation. The United States does not have any federal law prohibiting discrimination based on sexual orientation. And whereas U.S. federal age discrimination law applies only to people who are at least age forty, the EU directive protects both younger and older workers from discrimination based on age.

Why, then, do so many people believe that the United States has such an unfavorable climate for employers? One answer is the amount of ambiguity in U.S. employment law. Much of the lack of clarity comes about because of flexible doctrines such as the public policy exception to employment-at-will and the variation in state law. At each end of the spectrum of reasons for firing an employee, U.S. law is actually similar to that of other industrialized nations. It is legal to fire an employee for cause, such as for embezzling from the employer. It is never legal to fire an employee for reasons that the law defines as illegal discrimination. Where the laws differ is in cases where you, as a manager, are exercising significant discretion.

Return once again to the situation with Wendy. In many developed countries you either could not fire Wendy at all or you would need to give her significant notice and separation pay. In contrast, in the United States the only significant concern for you as a manager is whether the applicable state law protects Wendy's behavior outside the workplace. The newness of those laws and the uniqueness of Wendy's situation may mean that the answer is somewhat uncertain. If you wish to fire Wendy, it will make sense for you to obtain the advice of legal counsel in your state. While this ambiguity may be troubling, once managers understand the flexibility that the U.S. concept of employment-at-will gives them, they realize the benefits of that concept as compared to the heavy strictures in the legal landscape of many other developed countries.

■ Unique Features of the U.S. Legal System

Another reason that some people give for believing that the United States has an unfavorable employment law climate for employers is the nature of the U.S. legal system. It is true that the structure of the legal system adds increased risk to the ambiguity already imposed by laws that are unclear in their application and that vary from state to state. This section discusses some of the unique features of the legal system that you need to take into account as you make employment-related decisions.

■ Fact or Fallacy? ■

---

1. If an employee sues you and loses, the employee will have legal fees to pay.   ☐ Fact   ☐ Fallacy

2. The most you can lose in an employment lawsuit is the amount the company would have paid the employee in salary and benefits if the employee had not been illegally fired, denied promotion, or whatever.   ☐ Fact   ☐ Fallacy

3. Juries are overly sympathetic to plaintiff claims, and appealing a jury decision is unlikely to be of much help to a company.   ☐ Fact   ☐ Fallacy

4. Increasingly, employers are bypassing the U.S. court system when they face employment law claims.   ☐ Fact   ☐ Fallacy

Contingent Fees

The first threshold that a potential plaintiff needs to overcome is hiring a lawyer. From an economic perspective, it would make some sense if an employee who feels wronged had to weigh the strength of the claim and the size of the expected recovery against the cost of paying an attorney. Many plaintiffs' lawyers, however, accept employment law cases on what is known as a *contingent fee* basis. That means that if the lawyer is able to win a case or negotiate a settlement on behalf of the plaintiff, then the lawyer will get a percentage, typically about a third, of the award or settlement. If the lawyer is unsuccessful in represent-ing the individual, the plaintiff has little or no obligation to pay the lawyer beyond relatively small costs such as court filing fees.

From your perspective as a manager, this system means that a disgruntled employee will not face the costs of paying a lawyer if a legal claim is unsuccessful. Monetarily then, there is little to discourage one of your employees or former employees from pursuing a weak claim. On the other hand, it is in the in-terest of plaintiffs' lawyers to evaluate the strength of potential cases. It would not make much sense for a lawyer to invest the significant amounts of time and resources necessary to see a case through trial, and potentially through the appeal process, only to lose the case and not receive any compensation.

Two real-world factors affect the analysis of plaintiffs' lawyers, though. First, even in a weak case, a lawyer may be able to negotiate a quick settlement. Second, lawyers who are just getting started in practice, or who are temporarily under-employed for some reason, may be willing to accept relatively weak cases because having even weak cases is better than hav-ing no cases at all.

While the availability of contingent fees increases the like-lihood that you might be sued by a disgruntled employee with a tenuous legal case, public policy does support those fees. Cer-tainly some employees are fired, discriminated against in salary, or otherwise mistreated at work in ways that we all agree are and should be illegal. No one in this country suggests that children should be chained to machines and forced to work. Few managers would argue that the minimum wage laws should not be enforced against a competing company. However, enforcement of employment laws largely relies on claims by employees. Many employees, particularly the low-paid employees who might be most vulnerable to mistreatment, would not be able to afford the up-front costs of hiring a lawyer. In the absence of a contingent fee system, then, many clearly illegal employer actions might go unchallenged.

As a result, Fact or Fallacy? item 1 is a fallacy. The contingent fee system makes it relatively easy for a disgruntled worker or job applicant to sue without having the money in hand to pay a lawyer. Many managers object to this system because it means that individuals take very little risk in suing a company for an employment-related claim, particularly if they were not hired at that company or have been fired. On the other hand, supporters of the contingent fee system argue that it plays an important role in ensuring that people in the United States have access to the legal system.

Punitive Damages

An important factor to consider in evaluating any potential legal claim is the scope of possible damages you would have to pay if you lost. In an employment law case, a court may award a whole variety of damages, including reinstatement to a job, back pay, front pay, the employee's costs of finding a substitute job, emotional damages, and punitive damages.

It is the potential availability of punitive damages that makes Fact or Fallacy? item 2 a fallacy. Indeed, the size of some well-publicized punitive damage awards, which can run into tens and sometimes even hundreds of millions of dollars, is a major reason why this type of damages has received so much notoriety—and why it is of particular concern to corporate defendants.

While punitive damages often get bad press, it is important to realize why they exist: they are intended to punish defendants who have acted egregiously and to discourage them and others from engaging in the illegal conduct in the future. That said, many areas of the law put no caps on punitive damages and the amount of damages may be unrelated to the actual harm experienced by the plaintiff.

The law limits the availability of punitive damages to employment law plaintiffs in some circumstances. Under federal nondiscrimination law, a plaintiff can recover punitive damages only when the employer intentionally discriminates and does so either maliciously or with reckless indifference. Even when an employer's conduct is that wrongful, the law limits the punitive damages in many cases depending on the size of the employer. For small employers the cap is $50,000. Awards against employers with more than five hundred employees can total up to $300,000. Caps may not apply, however, in cases of race or national origin discrimination. Furthermore, some states permit either higher levels of punitive damages or uncapped damages. For example, the jury award of $10 million in favor of Phillip McConkey, discussed earlier in the chapter, was based on state law. So was the Iowa judgment of $80 million in the retaliation case I discussed.

Jury Decisions and Appellate Review

Many people in the United States believe that juries are likely to be sympathetic with individual plaintiffs when they sue large corporations. All of us are familiar with the notion that companies are viewed as having "deep pockets" and that those pockets are like piggy banks waiting to be smashed by successful plaintiffs. So it is not unusual for managers to believe that Fact or

Fallacy? item 3 is true. But cases show that juries do not always take the plaintiff's side, even when the plaintiff is sympathetic. Furthermore, one recent study indicates that juries may be even less likely than judges are to give large punitive damage awards. Finally, the statistics about appeals in some types of employment law cases tend to surprise people.

To show that juries do not always take the side of a sympathetic plaintiff, consider another case brought against Wal-Mart. Shirley Gasper worked at a Wal-Mart store in Nebraska developing customer photographs. When Ms. Gasper noticed a picture that seemed to show a bruised infant crawling in a pile of marijuana with $50 and $100 bills scattered around the edges of the photograph, she turned the photograph over to the police without obtaining permission from the customer or her supervisor, who was out of town and could not view the pictures. The police praised her decision, but Wal-Mart fired her because her actions violated the company's policy of confidentiality for customer photographs. Ms. Gasper sued Wal-Mart, alleging that her firing violated public policy.

At least superficially, Ms. Gasper would seem to be a sympathetic plaintiff. After all, she did not get any personal gain from turning the photo over to the police. She believed she had a duty to report what she viewed as possible evidence of child abuse. Furthermore, Wal-Mart certainly fits the profile of a deep-pocketed defendant. Nevertheless, the Nebraska jury decided in Wal-Mart's favor, and the appellate court also found for Wal-Mart. It seems likely that Wal-Mart persuaded the jury that Ms. Gasper should have discussed the pictures with a higher level of store management rather than taking it upon herself to violate the company's confidentiality policy.

When an employer does lose an employment law case at trial, a recent study of cases of employment discrimination indicates it may be in the employer's best interest to appeal. The study determined that when employers lost at trial and appealed, they won their appeal almost 44 percent of the time. In contrast, when the employer won at trial and the employee appealed, less than 6 percent of those appeals resulted in reversals in the employee's favor. These statistics are in stark contrast to the averages for all categories of appeals in federal courts. On average, when defendants lose at trial, they succeed on appeal only about 33 percent of the time, significantly less than the rate for employers in employment discrimination cases. And, when plaintiffs lose at trial, they succeed on appeal about 12 percent of the time, or about twice the rate of plaintiffs in employment discrimination cases.[9]

The study did not attempt to explain why the statistics in these employment law cases are so much more favorable for employers than the overall statistics are for other categories of defendants. Still, the results should be encouraging to managers who fear that the court system may look at companies as deep pockets.

In sum, neither the jury system nor the appellate process may be as weighted against employers as many managers fear. Nevertheless, the realistic manager will consider the nature of the system when making any employment-related decision. Even if you have complied with all the technical legal requirements, do you want to risk explaining your actions to a judge or a jury where those actions might appear harsh, unfair, or arbitrary? On the other hand, would you feel more comfortable explaining your decision to fire an incompetent employee after you have counseled and warned that employee?

Avoiding the Court System

Many managers view the U.S. court system's role in employment disputes as a necessary evil—something akin to an occupational hazard that cannot be avoided and must be dealt with. Thus, Fact or Fallacy? item 4 is true because employers are using arbitration and other nonadjudicative approaches to resolve disputes. In March 2001 the U.S. Supreme Court ruled that employers can enforce arbitration agreements against their employees.

Why do managers view arbitration as being a better way than the court system to resolve employment law disputes? There are several reasons. To begin with, managers often want to get employment disputes behind them and not wait years and years for the case to work its way through the courts. Arbitration cases can be heard more quickly and less expensively than a case that goes to trial, let alone one that proceeds to appeal. Furthermore, almost all court proceedings and written decisions are available to the public. As a result, managers often fear, quite reasonably, that even an employment law claim that has no basis in fact can damage the manager's and the company's reputation. In contrast, arbitration proceedings can be kept confidential, as can any written decision rendered by the arbitrator. Finally, many arbitration policies specify that arbitration is binding. In the absence of very unusual circumstances, such as bribery of the arbitrator, a decision in a binding arbitration case is final and cannot be appealed, a fact that saves both time and money.

Because arbitration has numerous advantages, companies are showing interest in requiring employees to arbitrate employment law disputes. For example, Sears, Roebuck recently began a new method of resolving disputes for almost sixteen thousand employees at two of its businesses. That method encourages employees to start by attempting to settle their disputes at a local level. Ultimately, if nothing else is successful, the process culminates in binding arbitration. Historically Sears has spent more money on legal costs for employment-related disputes than on any other type of legal issues.[10] The company hopes that the use of this new process, including binding arbitration, will decrease those costs.

Some open questions on employer-mandated arbitration policies remain and some people believe that it is unfair to require employees to arbitrate their claims. For example, some employers require employees to share the costs of paying for the arbitration. Those costs can climb into the thousands of dollars. Some courts have refused to enforce those cost-sharing requirements on the grounds that they act to discourage employees from pursuing their rights. The employees would not face similar costs in courts. For example, after he had a seizure at work, Waffle House fired Eric Baker, a grill cook who made $5.50 an hour. Rather than file for arbitration, Mr. Baker took his complaint that Waffle House had illegally discriminated against him because of a disability to the federal Equal Employment Opportunity Commission (EEOC). The EEOC has the power to seek enforcement of the federal nondiscrimination laws. The EEOC took interest in his claim and sued Waffle House on Mr. Baker's behalf. The U.S. Supreme Court decided, in 2002, that even if Mr. Baker had signed an enforceable arbitration agreement with Waffle House, that agreement could not prevent the EEOC from suing on his behalf.

Arbitration is not yet a standard with U.S. employers. Other issues remain, in addition to the question of whether employers may require employees to share the costs of arbitration. How significantly can an employer limit an employee's right to discovery? Who should choose the arbitrators? May an employer's policy limit the damages that an arbitrator can award? In spite of the gray areas, though, arbitration and other methods of alternative dispute resolution offer employers some opportunity to avoid the costs of lengthy litigation.

■ Recognizing Employment Law Issues as a Business Risk

As a manager, you should analyze employment-related issues as you do any other business problem: as both posing risks and offering rewards. Too often I see managers who are paralyzed by the fear of an employment lawsuit even though the same managers recognize and accept that they cannot completely avoid the risk of other types of lawsuits. For example, any manager involved with product development, design, or manufacture knows that it is impossible to guarantee that no customer will ever file a product liability lawsuit. Some lawsuits may be brought by customers who unreasonably misused the product or who otherwise have a very weak legal case. Additionally, some of those lawsuits, even the weak ones, may damage the company's reputation. But without products the company would be out of business, so accepting some risk of a lawsuit is critical to the continuing success of the company. The best managers not only recognize this fact but bring all of their own professional expertise to bear on their jobs. They seek outside advice from lawyers and other experts on how to minimize risks within the design and manufacturing parameters they establish.

I encourage you to view employment-related issues similarly. No business can maximize its potential unless it can hire outstanding employees, motivate its workforce, and fire incompetent employees. As you pursue excellence in your workforce, though, no one can guarantee that you will not be sued by a disgruntled job candidate, employee, or ex-employee. Nor can anyone promise that a weak lawsuit will not impose costs on your company in terms of time, money, or reputation.

Avoiding all potential employment law cases, however, is as unrealistic as avoiding all product liability cases. There will be times when you decide that the risks involved in addressing problems are well worth the potential rewards of improving the quality and morale of your workforce.

In addition, I believe that legal standards very typically are consistent with good management. As you set your moral compass for interactions with your employees, using common sense, consideration, fairness, and thinking through the implications of your actions often will help ensure that you are in compliance with relevant laws. After all, laws tend to reflect societal values.

So by connecting with those values, not only will you be complying with the law, you will be actively preventing legal issues from arising. It will also help avoid situations where you may be in legal compliance with the law, but your actions appear so unreasonable or harsh that you and your company face bad publicity or lose a jury verdict because of negative perceptions.

In closing this introductory chapter, let me emphasize that this book is not intended to be a substitute for the intense training involved in a legal education. It does not give legal advice, nor does it cover the myriad of state and federal laws that can affect a final employment-related decision. Instead, it gives you a basic understanding of the fundamental concepts of U.S. employment law, which are no less important to you as a manager than a base knowledge of accounting, finance, or marketing. From there you will be better prepared to discuss with the relevant experts the specific issues you encounter with your workforce, and you'll have a better idea of when to seek expert help.

One last time, consider the opening situation with Wendy. Upon learning of Wendy's involvement in the Web site, as Wendy's manager you have three options. First, you can be so fearful of an employment lawsuit that you decide to take no action at all. Second, you can react immediately and fire Wendy. Each of these actions reflects an extreme position and poses risk for you as a manager. In the first instance, you may confront serious problems from concerned parents of other children counseled by Wendy, the possibility of negative publicity for the counseling program, and even potential harm to the children if the children's access to the Web site somehow undercuts Wendy's effectiveness as a counselor. In the second option, a hasty decision to fire Wendy may leave open the possibility of a lawsuit whose risks you have not fully evaluated. A third approach would be to consider the situation using the basic principles of employment-at-will, the exceptions to employment-at-will, and the discussion of terminating employees in Chapter Six. This analysis would raise a variety of specific questions, which you could then pose, if needed, to the appropriate person in your human resources department or to a lawyer. This, of course, is a wiser approach, and it is the one that this book will enable you to adopt.

CHAPTER SUMMARY

The most basic concept in U.S. employment law is employment-at-will, which permits you, as a manager, to fire (or not hire or not promote) someone for any reason, even a lousy or arbitrary reason, so long as it is not an illegal reason.

There are three basic categories of exceptions to employment-at-will: contractual, nondiscrimination, and public policy and local statutory exceptions. Even allowing for those exceptions, a comparison of the U.S. approach with that taken in other industrialized countries shows that managers in the United States have considerable ability to select and motivate an exceptional workforce.

The nature of the U.S. legal system poses some specific challenges for employers and managers, including the availability of contingent fees and punitive damages. Nevertheless, the U.S. legal system is less weighted against employers than many managers believe. In addition, some companies are attempting to avoid or decrease the costs associated with employment litigation by establishing alternative dispute resolution policies. Typically those policies culminate in binding arbitration, which can limit publicity, cost, time, and acrimony.

As a manager, you should approach the legal aspects of employment questions as you do other business problems, as posing both benefits and risk. The mere possibility of a lawsuit should not determine your decisions; instead, you should carefully weigh risks and rewards, just as you do when confronted with other issues. By setting your internal compass to treat employees fairly, thoughtfully, and with consideration, most of the time you will also place yourself in compliance with legal standards. My goal in this book is to provide you with a base of knowledge so that you can best use the appropriate experts, engage lawyers productively to assist in analyzing your problems when necessary, and, ultimately, protect both yourself and your company while you build the best possible workforce.

Selecting Employees

C onsider the situation that Kevin faces as manager of product development at a midsize engineering company. Over the past few years, he has seen his department reduced in size as a result of retirements and layoffs. Finally, the company has turned the corner and his area's workload has increased dramatically. Kevin just received approval to hire an additional engineer for product development. He could use three more people, but one is better than none. Kevin knows, though, that he needs to make the most of this hiring opportunity. He is young, relatively new in his managerial position, and has not done much hiring.

2

Selecting Employees

C onsider the situation that Kevin faces as manager of product development at a midsize engineering company. Over the past few years, he has seen his department reduced in size as a result of retirements and layoffs. Finally, the company has turned the corner and his area's workload has increased dramatically. Kevin just received approval to hire an additional engineer for product development. He could use three more people, but one is better than none. Kevin knows, though, that he needs to make the most of this hiring opportunity. He is young, relatively new in his managerial position, and has not done much hiring.

29

In this chapter, I discuss the legal environment facing a manager such as Kevin. While the examples I use focus on hiring new employees, similar considerations apply if you are selecting an internal candidate for promotion. In each case, the most significant legal risk is that you might be sued by an individual who believes you discriminated based on a prohibited criterion during the selection process.

In addition to identifying and interviewing job candidates, I address some other key issues such as testing applicants, doing background checks, and ensuring that the chosen candidate is legally entitled to work in the United States. While some of these functions might be handled at your company by a human resources department, as a manager you should understand how they fit within the employee selection process.

The good news for you as a manager is that the concept of employment-at-will applies to hiring and promoting employees. You are legally entitled to select an employee for any reason at all, even a lousy or arbitrary reason, so long as your choice is not affected by an illegal consideration. Of course, like Kevin, most managers are anxious to hire the best possible employee. As you will see, being aware of potential legal risks can actually help you achieve that result.

■ Fact or Fallacy? ■

1. Job descriptions should be as general as possible to maintain management flexibility in assigning work.   □ Fact   □ Fallacy

2. In looking for suitable candidates for an opening, it's unwise to rely only on sources you know well, such as existing employees, your religious institution, or your college.   □ Fact   □ Fallacy

---

■ Fact or Fallacy?, Cont'd ■

---

3. There is a specific list of questions that it is illegal to ask during a job interview, but so long as you do not ask any of those questions, all other subjects are OK.   □ Fact   □ Fallacy

4. If it becomes clear in the first five minutes of a scheduled half-hour interview that the candidate is not viable, you should nevertheless proceed with the entire interview.   □ Fact   □ Fallacy

5. You should not keep notes of your interviews because those notes might be used against you in court.   □ Fact   □ Fallacy

---

■ Defining the Job and Identifying Candidates

Once Kevin receives authorization to hire, he faces two critical tasks. First, he must define the duties of the open position and the minimum requirements of candidates. Second, he must decide how and where to seek applicants. In addition to helping Kevin meet his goal of hiring the best possible employee, performing these two tasks well will help ensure that he complies with relevant nondiscrimination laws. As you will see throughout this book, it's often the case that making efforts to ensure that you comply with the law can also help you achieve your business objectives.

Writing a Job Description

When defining the duties of the engineering position, Kevin must analyze the necessary functions of the position and how the job fits within the department and the company. Many managers believe that job descriptions should be as general as possible to maintain management flexibility in assigning work (Fact or Fallacy? item 1), but this belief is a fallacy. At the very least, a carefully drafted description of the job's requirements can eliminate miscommunications and misunderstandings between the manager and the candidates (and the eventual hire). It will also provide a basis for the manager to use in establishing any minimum education and work criteria. After all, even if Kevin's department is engaged in the engineering of a new product, the open job may not require an engineering degree. Or perhaps, once the description is written, Kevin will realize that the candidate must have a Ph.D. in mechanical engineering. Finally, as I discuss further in Chapter Four, a description of essential functions also permits the manager to evaluate whether disabled applicants are able, with or without reasonable accommodation, to perform those functions.

This last point can be particularly important from a legal perspective. In determining whether a candidate has the physical ability to perform the essential functions of the job, courts typically defer to the essential functions set forth in the job description. It is necessary, though, that the description contain sufficient detail to determine exactly what the physical requirements are. If the job description is too general, then management forfeits this deference.

Soliciting Applicants

Obviously, the method Kevin uses to solicit applicants will have a significant effect on the nature of the candidate pool. For example, Kevin might avoid the hassle and expense of advertising the open position or engaging in other proactive recruiting efforts by hiring Michael, an engineer Kevin knows from his evening softball league.

Such an approach has some positive aspects, but it also carries some risk. On the positive side, Kevin is reasonably well acquainted with Michael, knows there are unlikely to be serious personality clashes between the two of them, and has an idea of how Michael would fit into the dynamics of the department. On the other hand, in its report on *Best Practices of Private Sector Employers*, the federal Equal Employment Opportunity Commission recognized that the "Like Me" syndrome is a serious barrier to equal job opportunity.[1] The "Like Me" syndrome is the tendency of managers to hire people they perceive as similar to themselves. Those are the people the manager may be most comfortable with. They may be the most readily known candidates. They may be members of the same religious institution, graduates of the same alma mater, or neighbors of the manager or of other departmental employees. For example, Kevin may be tempted to see if he can fill his position through the placement office or alumni association of his university, or by asking his colleagues about people they know. In the worst case, the "Like Me" syndrome leads a manager to discriminate against candidates based on prohibited criteria. As I will explain later in this chapter, even unintentional discrimination can violate the law.

No law requires the typical employer to use any specific recruiting methods. To obtain a broad applicant pool and achieve a diverse workforce, which also reflects their customer base, many employers take proactive steps in advertising open positions and recruiting employees. For example, Kevin might announce the opening in a variety of general and specialized professional journals, schedule interviews at a range of universities, or use a job search firm.

To sum up, many companies do successfully recruit new employees by working familiar networks. It can be unwise, however, to rely on such limited methods of recruiting (Fact or Fallacy? item 2) because you run a serious risk of ending up with a one-dimensional workforce lacking in diversity. Not only can that result in legal issues, it may mean that the company forfeits a richness of diversity in viewpoints, experience, and education.

■ Interviewing Candidates

Once a manager has identified promising job candidates, the next step typically is to conduct personal interviews. In addition to obtaining the information necessary to make a good hiring decision, job interviewers need to be aware of a variety of potential legal pitfalls. In this section, I discuss three of those pitfalls: inappropriate or illegal questions; high-risk time periods during the interview; and note taking.

Questions During Interviews

As a manager, you can access a great deal of very specific guidance on what questions you may and may not ask when interviewing job candidates. Many employers also provide their managers and human resources professionals with training or guidance on interviewing practices. As with all discussions in this book, I recommend that you familiarize yourself with company practices and take pains to follow them. Not only will that help ensure that you meet your company's expectations, it will also help maintain consistency within the company. That consistency can be critical in avoiding liability for prohibited discrimination.

Here I want to focus on the logic behind limits on what you may ask during an interview. As I mentioned in Chapter One, state and federal laws prohibit managers from making job-related decisions based on specific prohibited criteria, such as gender, race, religion, color, or national origin. It is therefore understandable that the law would prohibit questions specifically designed to elicit information about these characteristics.

Many interview questions, while not specifically prohibited, raise more subtle concerns. For example, in interviewing Ernestine King for a position in Trans World Airlines' dining and commissary department, the manager of the department asked Ernestine a variety of personal questions. The questions included "the number of children she had and whether they were illegitimate, her childcare arrangements, and her future child-bearing plans."[2] After TWA hired ten or eleven people, but not her, Ernestine brought a lawsuit against TWA alleging gender and race discrimination. TWA admitted that other job candidates were not asked about childcare and related family issues during their interviews. As a result, the court decided that it appeared TWA had treated Ernestine differently, in part at least, because of unlawful discrimination.

Cases such as Ernestine's are a reminder that our beliefs and stereotypes can cause serious problems in an interviewing situation. For example, suppose Kevin believes that women who have small children are prone to miss work. He may even have had an issue in the past with a female employee whose work suffered because of childcare problems. If he then asks women applicants about their childcare arrangements, he could properly point out that "childcare arrangements" is not a criterion that federal or state law prohibits him from taking into account when making an employment decision. Even Michigan's long list of prohibited questions does not refer to childcare. But if Kevin asks only female job candidates about their plans for childcare, he has treated the female candidates differently from male candidates in the interviewing process. That risks legal action by an unsuccessful female candidate.

In sum, most managers are aware that state and federal employment-related laws limit what questions they may ask job candidates. It is a fallacy to believe, though, that any specific list of forbidden questions is complete and that it is safe to ask any questions not on such a list (Fact or Fallacy? item 3).

As you confront new issues and develop your internal compass in this area, keep three general principles in mind. First, none of your questions should be designed to obtain information about criteria such as national origin on which it would be illegal for you to base an employment decision. Second, you should be sure to stay up to date with your company's policies regarding interviewing. Third, to the extent reasonably possible, you should treat all job candidates consistently.

Risk Points During Interviews

In addition to keeping in mind the specific concerns with inappropriate questions, Kevin will want to pay particular attention to his conversation with candidates during the beginning and the end of each interview. These two time periods raise particular risks. Often during the initial few minutes, an interviewer will make an effort to put the job candidate at ease. Many of us connect with other people by discussing mutual interests such as family, hobbies, or community activities. Unfortunately, many of those same topics can lead to the types of personal questions and conversations that are prohibited. For example, Kevin might notice that Beryl, a job candidate, lives in his neighborhood. To put her at ease, he might refer to the neighborhood and ask if she has children who go to the local elementary school. Kevin could view this as social chit-chat. Beryl, however, may perceive this as a way for Kevin to ask about her family status and whether she has children. This could become particularly problematic if Kevin uses a different type of opening conversation, perhaps about local sports teams, when talking with male applicants. Similarly, it may feel natural to close the interview with some general chit-chat. Again, however, to the extent that this informal conversation involves personal matters, it can stray into topics that relate to discriminatory decision criteria. Interviews that extend into mealtimes pose the same risk.

The safest course is to keep the interview focused on the criteria for the job. Another book in this series, *Strategic Interviewing* by Richaurd Camp, Mary Vielhaber, and Jack Simonetti, does an excellent job of discussing techniques for conducting job interviews and selecting employees. By concentrating on the elements of the position description and on each candidate's qualifications, you will avoid legal liability while maximizing the likelihood that you will hire the best possible candidate.

Another hazard arises when you become convinced during the first few minutes of an interview that the candidate is not viable. Should you immediately terminate the interview, as many managers believe? Or should you proceed with the entire interview anyway? (Fact or Fallacy? item 4.)

Immediately terminating the interview poses two risks. First, some excellent candidates may be so nervous or shy during the first few minutes of an interview that your initial impression is not at all consistent with their skills. For some jobs, first impressions may be critical. But for other jobs, a manager who conducts the entire interview may discover an exceptionally qualified candidate. Second, from a legal perspective it is important to treat candidates consistently and give everyone a fair opportunity.

Put yourself in the shoes of the typical candidate. You have prepared carefully, driven to an unfamiliar location, and endured all the stress that most people experience before an interview. You know the interview is scheduled for a half-hour, yet the manager dismisses you after five minutes. You probably leave that situation with a negative impression of the manager and the company. The negative perception alone may be problematic if you are a customer, have future dealings with the manager, or otherwise come within six degrees of separation of the company. If you learn later that the manager has a pattern of dismissing certain types of candidates after five minutes—for example, members of a specific race, gender, or religion—you may be inclined to sue alleging discrimination. And, based on the apparent pattern, you may have a reasonable claim.

Note Taking During Interviews

Managers I have talked with over the years follow two very different approaches to keeping records of job interviews. Some companies have a policy that interviewers should minimize the notes they take during an interview and destroy any notes after a hiring decision is finalized. The theory behind those policies is that the notes are useful only in selecting a candidate for a particular opening at a particular point in time. Because the notes serve no continuing purpose, there is no business reason to maintain them and they should be destroyed. A corollary benefit is that if there is any litigation over the hiring process, such as a charge of discrimination by a disappointed candidate, the notes cannot be used against the company or manager.

In contrast, other companies encourage interviewers to make and retain a record of the interviewing and decision-making process. This type of policy has a number of benefits. First, the discipline of keeping a written record, often on a company-developed form, can assist you in distinguishing among candidates and in making a reasoned decision. Second, if litigation does occur, the written records can help you refresh your memory and be effective in explaining your decision-making process. The very fact that you have documentation reflecting a careful process may be compelling to a judge or jury evaluating the credibility of your explanations.

Finally, recent events, such as those that occurred at Enron, have made many of us more sensitive to both the legal issues and the public perceptions associated with destroying documents. As a general matter, it may be illegal to destroy documents when litigation is pending or reasonably foreseeable. Furthermore, a variety of federal and state employment law regulations require that personnel records be kept for between one and thirty years, and some of these regulations may apply to interviewing records.

The situation of a school in Connecticut serves as a good example of how the failure to keep interviewing documentation can be problematic. The school chose to hire a relatively young female art teacher over an older male, Robert Byrnie, who had numerous years of experience. Byrnie sued, alleging that the school had discriminated against him based on age and gender. Consistent with the school's policy and routine process, all the documents related to the job search had been destroyed. Given the other facts in the case, the court decided that "enough circumstantial evidence exist[ed] to permit a reasonable trier of fact to conclude that the destroyed documents would show unlawful discrimination."[3] In plain English, the court was saying that Byrnie would be permitted to make his case of discrimination to a jury. He would be allowed to argue that the jury should infer from the destruction of the documents that they would have shown unlawful discrimination.

The court in this case did not discuss in any detail the extent to which the applicable regulations require an employer to maintain interview notes and rankings of job candidates. This is an area in which the law is somewhat unclear. Another court has taken a practical approach and said, "Employers are not required to keep every single piece of scrap paper that various employees may create during the [employment-related decision process.]"[4]

The bottom line for the Fact or Fallacy? statement about note taking is that you should make sure that any notes you take during an interview, or during meetings that occur as part of a hiring decision, refer only to job-related criteria. For example, if a candidate's religion is irrelevant to the job, then your notes should not refer to religion even if the candidate brings it up during the interview or lists it on a résumé. After the hiring process is complete, you should follow your company's procedures on document retention. Be aware, however, that destruction of documents can be damaging. Sometimes the most convincing document is the one that has been shredded.

■ Selecting the Top Candidate

After using the interviewing process to select a new employee, the next major step typically is to screen the preferred candidate or candidates. Here I will discuss three key elements of screening that may invoke legal issues: testing, background checks, and determining that a candidate is eligible to work in the United States.

■ Fact or Fallacy? ■

1. Testing applicants' skills to screen out people who could not perform the job can sometimes create legal hazards for the company.   ☐ Fact   ☐ Fallacy

2. It is never legal to give applicants a personality test.   ☐ Fact   ☐ Fallacy

3. It is useless to check an applicant's work references because employers so rarely provide any information other than basic facts.   ☐ Fact   ☐ Fallacy

4. The fact that an applicant has been arrested or convicted of a misdemeanor may be an insufficient reason to refuse to hire the applicant.   ☐ Fact   ☐ Fallacy

5. If an applicant has a Social Security card, that is sufficient evidence of a legal right to work in the United States.   ☐ Fact   ☐ Fallacy

---

Testing Applicants

The tragic events of September 11, 2001, seem to have reawakened managers' interest in workplace testing, particularly in personality testing, and in background checks. Kevin, for example, does not want to hire someone who might become violent or sabotage any of the company's products. Testing job applicants can be useful, but even skills testing has the potential to raise a variety of legal issues. Thus, Fact or Fallacy? item 1 is true. Before addressing those issues, it is useful to briefly outline the different types of tests used in employment decisions.

Employment tests can be grouped into four broad categories: personality or attitudinal, cognitive or simulation, drug, and medical. Managers who want to screen out applicants who have poor attitudes, who might be violent, or who are particular risks for committing other security violations may be most interested in using personality tests. Tests that assess honesty and integrity are a subset of more generalized personality tests.

Cognitive and simulation tests concentrate on a candidate's intellectual or job skills. Cognitive tests frequently cover areas such as reading retention, math or other quantitative skills, or written and verbal communication ability.

Simulation testing typically involves putting candidates into an environment similar to the workplace and asking them to perform tasks like those of the open position. One large automotive company uses simulation testing when hiring engineers. Applicants are given relevant memoranda describing engineering issues and an office with a phone and computer. They must then evaluate the issues, schedule appropriate meetings, and so forth.

Drug testing is preemployment testing of a very different sort. While the concept is obvious, implementation of a drug testing program may take many different forms. Urinalysis, for instance, measures chemicals that have been in the body for a relatively short time. In comparison, testing of a strand of hair from a person with long hair can identify drug use that occurred in the somewhat distant past. There is even some evidence that hair testing can reflect secondhand exposure. The hair of children who never took drugs but who were in homes where crack was smoked sometimes reflects exposure to the crack. An employer that institutes a drug testing program must consider whether the testing will identify drug use that is of concern and must determine what drugs it will screen for.

Finally, some companies require a physical examination before a candidate can be hired. It is important to note that employers can require a physical exam only after the candidate has received a conditional job offer.

All four types of preemployment testing can raise a variety of legal risks. Here, I will describe three kinds of concerns: privacy rights, nondiscrimination laws, and the specific prohibitions of the Americans with Disability Act.

Privacy Rights

Some types of preemployment testing raise issues of violations of privacy. For example, psychological testing may provide managers with insights into an applicant's character and personality that are impossible to obtain during a traditional interview. However, the penetrating nature of many psychological tests causes them to be at particular risk for charges of invasion of privacy. Reportedly, Target stores settled a class action lawsuit of this type brought by candidates for security guard positions for more than a million dollars. Rent-A-Center paid more than two million dollars to settle allegations that its use of a fairly standard personality test violated the applicants' rights to privacy.[5] Both cases were brought in California, which is one of a limited number of states where the state constitution contains personal privacy protections. The scope of protection provided in other states is less clear, but most, if not all, provide at least some individual privacy rights. Thus managers should carefully investigate the use of personality tests or other similar tests that address concerns with morality or integrity. Contrary to Fact or Fallacy? item 2, however, personality tests are not illegal in and of themselves.

Privacy concerns are also associated with drug testing. As with personality tests, the relevant law applied to private employers tends to be state or local law, and the law varies significantly from one state to another. No state that I know of, however, currently bans all preemployment drug testing. In fact, permitting some drug testing is consistent with the federal Drug-Free Workplace Act. That law does not require private employers to engage in drug testing, but it does require government contractors to make good faith efforts to ensure that their workplaces are drug-free.

Even California, with its relatively extensive constitutional privacy protections, has upheld the right of nongovernmental employers to require job applicants to undergo drug testing. The California court that decided the relevant case recognized that employers have a legitimate interest in testing. In fact, some data indicate that approximately 10 percent of all employment drug tests return positive results for drug use.[6] Nevertheless, companies that implement preemployment drug testing should take steps to respect the privacy rights of job candidates and ensure the fairness of the tests. At minimum, an employer should give applicants notice of the testing, implement reasonable collection procedures, and ensure that the test results are safeguarded.[7] Some employers take the additional step of double-checking positive results either with a second sample or by using a different laboratory to perform a duplicate analysis.

Finally, the federal Employee Polygraph Protection Act and various state laws make it nearly impossible for most employers to require job applicants to take lie detector tests. You are also typically prohibited from asking about lie detector tests that the individual may have taken for other purposes. Under limited circumstances, you may be able to require a current employee to take a lie detector test, but the area is heavily enough regulated that you probably would want to talk to legal counsel about the specific situation and the required notifications that must be made to employees.

Nondiscrimination

Preemployment tests can also run afoul of nondiscrimination laws. Any of the four types of preemployment testing I have described may raise legal issues if the test in question has the *effect* of excluding disproportionately large numbers of a protected group. Not only is it illegal under federal law to intentionally discriminate against individuals based on a prohibited criterion, it can be illegal to use any screening device that has the effect of disqualifying members of a protected group at a significantly higher rate than members of a majority group. This theory of liability is known as "disparate impact" discrimination.

If a test has the statistical effect of violating the disparate impact standard, it is not automatically illegal. Instead the law permits employers to use testing methods that are necessary to accomplish their business objectives, provided the tests have been validated to ensure they meet that standard. This is not an easy standard to meet because often there are less discriminatory ways to assess candidates. The EEOC has provided guidance on how tests can be validated, and it takes the validation requirements seriously. One federal court recently upheld the EEOC's right to obtain copies of an employer's tests and validation studies in spite of the employer's argument that disclosure of the tests could nullify their usefulness.[8]

Once a test is appropriately validated, an employer may use it to screen candidates for relevant jobs even if the test does have a disparate impact on protected groups. For example, a federal court of appeals upheld California's use of a test for prospective teachers that measured basic math, writing, and reading skills even though the test had a disproportionate impact on Mexican American, Asian American, and African American applicants.[9]

The bottom line is that if a test has the effect of disqualifying job candidates who are members of a protected group at a substantially higher rate than majority group members, the test may violate nondiscrimination laws. If the test is challenged in court, the employer will need to show that the test accurately assesses whether a candidate can perform necessary job functions. And even an accurate test will not be legal if there is an alternative, less discriminatory test that would accomplish the same objective.

The Americans with Disabilities Act

The Americans with Disabilities Act forbids managers from discriminating against candidates who can perform the essential functions of a job with or without accommodation. If it is obvious that an applicant is disabled, then you may ask whether the applicant can perform the essential functions of the job, and you may ask whether any accommodation would be needed. It is also legal to ask such applicants to show how they would perform the job as evidence of their ability.

You are more restricted in what you may ask applicants who are not obviously disabled. You may ask all candidates whether they can perform the essential functions of the job with or without accommodation. You may not, however, ask the applicants who are not obviously disabled whether they have a disability or any physical limitations, or whether they would require any accommodations to perform the job. As with all assessment questions, the interviewer should be careful to ask the same questions of all candidates.

Finally, remember that an employer cannot require a job candidate to undergo a medical examination until after it has made a conditional offer of employment. In most situations that requirement is simple to implement. However, a psychological test that is given prior to an offer of employment and discloses a mental disability may violate this standard. And medical examinations must be consistent in their application to all new hires.

Conducting a Background Check

Assume Kevin has interviewed candidates and has decided on the best person for the open job. The threshold question he might be asking at this point is: "If I have carefully interviewed the applicants and made a hiring decision, why should I bother with a background check?" Unfortunately, plenty of recent situations show that dishonest applicants can fool even careful and sophisticated interviewers. Federal regulators accused Al Dunlop, Sunbeam's former CEO, of causing Sunbeam to engage in accounting fraud. A thorough background check would have warned Sunbeam that Dunlop had left two prior jobs off his résumé and he had been accused of accounting improprieties at one of those companies.[10] Notre Dame hired George O'Leary as the head coach for its vaunted football program. It took only a few days for the media to report that O'Leary had padded his résumé. He resigned before really beginning the job.[11] With due care, the university could have avoided the embarrassment this episode caused.

Even low-level employees can cause serious liability for employers that do not perform background checks. A Domino's Pizza franchise in Omaha, Nebraska, hired David Taitte, who claimed to have a good driving record. The franchise failed to check Taitte's record as required by Domino's policies. At minimum the check would have shown numerous driving violations. A thorough criminal check would have shown that Taitte had once been convicted of attempted first-degree sexual assault on a child. He also had been arrested for stalking a woman he met while working on another job as a pizza delivery driver. While delivering pizza for the Domino's franchise, Taitte raped a customer. She successfully sued the franchise and won $175,000.[12]

The legal concept typically used by plaintiffs in these types of cases is known as negligent hiring. The basic premise is that an employer must take reasonable actions in its hiring process to ensure the safety of its customers, suppliers, and other employees. There are no generally applicable laws that require employers to take specific actions to investigate a new employee's background. There are, however, some rules of thumb.

First, contrary to Fact or Fallacy? item 3, it is useful to verify a candidate's address and work history, even if, as is often the case, the reference will provide nothing more than basic facts. At least you have obtained confirmation that the individual did work at the places claimed for the relevant time periods. On the other hand, if you discover inconsistencies or gaps in the employment history, that should at least signal a concern with the candidate's credibility. It may be a sign of something far more insidious.

Depending on the job level of the potential employee and the person's interface with other employees, the public, or the possibility of something such as product tampering, you may want to undertake a more comprehensive background investigation. As with almost all employment-related actions, you want to ensure that the investigations are equivalent for all similarly situated candidates. A company that performs credit checks on all new female software developers, but not on the males, is leaving itself open to a charge of gender discrimination.

Employers can also turn to one of the many firms that perform a full range of background checking tasks, such as checks of credit history, criminal convictions, driving records, personal references, and job references. If you engage an outside firm to perform a background check on a potential or current employee, however, you must comply with a federal law known as the Fair Credit Reporting Act. The requirements of that Act are too detailed to go into here, but most generally, the Act requires you to inform candidates in writing that you will be hiring a third party to perform a background check. Candidates must then consent in writing to the background investigation. Other laws may affect the scope of the background check. For example, some states regulate inquiries into arrests and convictions.

Given the difficulty of obtaining detailed employment performance information from traditional sources, some managers have begun to use alternative methods. One technique is to ask job candidates to supply copies of performance appraisals from prior jobs. In many states, such as Michigan, employees have a legal right to see and copy documents in their employment files, including performance evaluations. Many employers provide copies of performance appraisals to employees as a matter of policy. Another technique borrows from the concept of 360-degree performance appraisals, which incorporate feedback from peers, customers, and subordinates in addition to the traditional evaluation by the person's manager. A hiring manager might ask a job candidate for references that include the same array of people. Peers, customers, or subordinates may be more willing to talk to a potential employer than a former manager would. As I have heard someone say, "Managers can often fool their bosses, but they find it a lot harder to fool the people who work for them."

Under no circumstances, however, should you ever contact anyone associated with the applicant's current employer without obtaining the applicant's written consent. Such a contact could create serious problems for applicants at their current workplace, especially if you ultimately hire someone else to fill your open position.

Responding to Negative Information

Suppose Kevin discovers some negative information during the background check of his top candidate, what action should he take? One approach would be for Kevin to reject that particular candidate and turn to a backup candidate. But, as is often the case, some legal pitfalls are associated with that approach.

First, if the Fair Credit Reporting Act applied to the background check that uncovered the negative information, then you need to consider the Act's requirements. If you decide not to hire a particular applicant, or to take an adverse action regarding an existing employee, based even in part on the information you learn from the investigation, then you must meet specific disclosure obligations to the individual involved. That gives the individual an opportunity to review the report and challenge any inaccurate information.

Second, you need to consider whether the negative information is such that it should have any effect on your employment decision. There are two issues here: being too conservative and running the risk of a discrimination complaint, and, on the other hand, protecting yourself in the event that you decide to hire someone with a problematic past.

With respect to the discrimination issue, the EEOC takes the position that excluding people from jobs simply because of an arrest record or misdemeanor conviction may result in illegal discrimination. Statistics show that members of some minority groups are arrested and convicted at higher percentage rates than apply to members of other racial groups. Therefore, if an employer automatically disqualifies everyone with an arrest or conviction record, it will disqualify minority group members at a disproportionately high rate. That means that the employer is at a risk of violating employment discrimination prohibitions under the disparate impact theory.

As I explained in the discussion of testing, an exception permits an employer to use screening criteria that have a disproportionate effect if the criteria are necessary to the proper functioning of the business and no other, less discriminatory, criteria would be effective. So if Kevin were faced with an applicant with a felony conviction record, he should consider a variety of factors. How long ago did the conviction occur? What has the individual's employment record been like since the conviction?

Is the substance of the conviction related to the job at issue? For example, a school district probably should refuse to hire a convicted pedophile for a job working with children. But if fear of legal liability prevented companies from ever hiring individuals with criminal convictions, society would have serious problems rehabilitating anyone. Thus, Fact or Fallacy? item 4 is true: a record of arrest or even conviction is insufficient in itself as a reason to automatically deny someone employment.

What if you go ahead with a hire despite problems in an applicant's history? Are you then liable if the person engages in harmful behavior? As a general matter, so long as your decision is informed and reasonable, you should receive some protection from liability even if the employee's future behavior is problematic. Consider the following example, which provides some insight into the protections and obligations associated with making a reasonable hiring decision when a manager knows of serious problems in a worker's history.

Randy Landin worked for Honeywell Inc. from 1977 to 1979. Landin was convicted of strangling a fellow Honeywell employee, Nancy Miller, and spent the years from 1979 to 1984 in prison. After his release, Landin reapplied at Honeywell. The company decided to give him a second chance and rehired him as a custodian. After Landin got involved in some workplace disputes, Honeywell transferred him twice. He ended up working on a maintenance crew with Kathleen Nesser and they became friends. When Nesser rejected Landin's romantic efforts, though, Landin became threatening. Shortly afterward, Landin killed Nesser with a shotgun in her driveway. Nesser's heirs sued Honeywell.

The court addressed two separate issues in the Nesser case. First, it determined that Honeywell was *not* liable for negligently hiring Landin. Honeywell had, on an informed basis, made a reasonable decision to give Landin a second chance in the position of maintenance worker where he had limited contacts with other people. Second, Honeywell *did* fall short with respect to negligent retention. Generally, that theory results in liability for an employer where the employer has knowingly and intentionally retained an employee with dangerous tendencies. In this situation, once Landin, a man Honeywell knew had been convicted of murdering a fellow employee, started to get into workplace confrontations, then Honeywell had an obligation to terminate Landin in order to protect the rest of its employees.[13]

To summarize Kevin's responsibilities in the introductory scenario, it is important in today's employment climate that he either conduct a background check on the new employee he has selected or ensure that someone in human resources undertakes that responsibility. Verifying the history of a new employee is part of a reasonable decision-making process for most jobs. So long as the company has conducted a prudent background check and made a careful evaluation of the results, it is likely to receive some protection from legal liability if the employee engages in violent or deceitful conduct.

In this area, as in others, the law encourages managers to take certain actions and may even delay an action such as a final hiring decision. In the longer term, however, the legal incentives align with the manager's interest in making the best possible hiring decision.

■ Determining Eligibility to Work in the United States

Once Kevin has selected the top candidate, Lyon, for the job and the background check is complete, Kevin will need to verify that Lyon is legally able to work in the United States. In addition to an increased interest in testing and background checks, the events of September 11, 2001, raised employer awareness of issues in hiring foreign nationals. In particular, Kevin will need to ensure that Lyon properly completes and provides documentation for an I-9

Form. Two additional issues that apply to certain circumstances are H-1B visas and export control laws.

First, every employee who is hired in the United States now must complete an I-9 Form. The purpose of the I-9 is to ensure that the individual has the legal right to work in the United States. The form sets forth a clear list of required documentation. Some people falsely believe that a Social Security card is sufficient (Fact or Fallacy? item 5), but it constitutes proof of the right to work only when it is used in combination with one of a specific set of documents listed on the I-9 itself, such as a state-issued driver's license. The employee must provide the necessary supporting documentation within the first three days of employment. Failure to comply with the I-9 requirements can result in fines, and in severe cases imprisonment, for the manager who signs the form on behalf of the company attesting that all documentation was provided. Legal penalties aside, as a matter of protecting their reputations and enhancing their security, this is one legal requirement that companies and individual managers should be concerned with.

When U.S. unemployment rates were particularly low, some companies, especially in sectors such as technology, turned to foreign nationals to fill openings. Often the companies hired those individuals on what are known as H-1B visas. Very generally, those visas permit employers to hire foreign nationals in "specialty occupations." The visa approval process is complex and involves both the Department of Labor and the Immigration and Naturalization Service. Furthermore, the hiring company accepts some financial obligation if it eventually terminates such employees; it must make it possible for the individuals to return to their home country.

One of the least well-known legal issues with foreign nationals involves the export control laws. Because those laws apply to knowledge as well as to goods and technology, a company may violate those controls merely by exposing a foreign national to protected technology. The law treats the employer's provision of knowledge as an illegal export to the employee's home country.

In short, managers must ensure that newly hired employees have the legal right to work in the United States. In limited circumstances, you may hire foreign nationals under a variety of visa programs, such as the H-1B program. Those visa plans raise very complex and technical issues and should be handled by a specialist. Similarly, if your company is involved in technology controlled by export laws, you must be attentive to the prohibitions on giving foreign nationals, even those who are your employees, access to information about that technology.

■ Making a Job Offer

Finally, Kevin has completed the background check on Lyon and knows she is eligible to work in the United States. Now, Kevin's management strategy needs to change. Instead of being a buyer winnowing through candidates, he is a seller who must convince Lyon to take the job. As he does that, Kevin needs to remember the concepts from Chapter One.

First, as you know, any promises Kevin makes to Lyon are likely to be enforceable. Whether the promises are verbal or written, if Lyon ultimately convinces a judge or jury that Kevin made them, they probably will be enforced. Similarly, Kevin needs to ensure he is honest in answering any questions that Lyon might have. Otherwise, as in the situation with Philip McConkey in Chapter One, inaccurate answers could lead to liability.

Although no law requires it, most employers seem to put job offers in writing. Many also require the new hire to accept the position by signing and returning the letter. Such an approach can ensure that there are no misunderstandings on key points such as salary, title, and important benefits. An offer letter would also give Kevin a good opportunity to make sure Lyon is clearly informed that she will be an employee-at-will. As

I noted in Chapter One, the offer letter at one high-technology company not only specifies and explains the employee's at-will status, but goes on to state that the only way this status can be modified is by a written agreement signed by both the employee and the company president. In addition to effectively highlighting the importance of the employment-at-will concept, the letter helps to ensure that recruiters or overly enthusiastic managers do not make enforceable promises of long-term employment.

Other appropriate topics for the offer letter, or for contemporaneous agreements, may be arbitration, trade secret, and noncompete clauses. Some managers worry that bringing up these issues at the time of a job offer might discourage the candidate from accepting the offer. There are some fallacies associated with that belief, though. In some states it is important that an employer provide consideration—that is, something of value—for an individual who enters into such an agreement. If an employer makes a job offer conditional on acceptance of terms that include arbitration, trade secret protection, or a noncompete clause, then the employer has indeed provided something of value (the job offer). But if the employer extends the job offer and then asks the employee to accept the same terms at a later date, it may be necessary to provide the employee with additional compensation. It is less costly, then, to enter into these agreements at the time of employment. In addition, the employer may need protection on these fronts as soon as an employee begins work. As a side note, the enforceability of these agreements varies by their terms and by the law of the relevant state.

■ Notifying Other Applicants

Many employers make it a matter of policy to notify other applicants once an open position has been filled. Although there is no legal requirement to do so, it is good management practice, not to mention a courtesy, to notify, at minimum, those candidates who received personal interviews. The applicants are then free to make other employment decisions, and interviewers are less likely to have to deal with awkward follow-up calls from applicants wondering about the status of their applications. In addition, appropriate notifications can help maintain the candidates' respect for the company. That may be important if a candidate becomes an applicant for a future position or has other relationships with the company, such as customer, supplier, or shareholder.

There are no specific legal rules about how to notify applicants who were not selected for a position, but you should observe the same kinds of principles that have run through this discussion so far: put the notification in writing, treat all similarly situated applicants in the same way, and make sure all communications are absolutely honest. Finally, it is my own view that it is enough to notify the applicant that you have selected another candidate. Getting into specific analysis regarding an applicant's interview or background typically is not required, nor is it likely to soften the applicant's disappointment.

CHAPTER SUMMARY

Making a hiring decision or promoting a candidate from within the company involves a number of legal issues as well as principles of good management practice. It is possible, though, to develop an internal compass to assist you in making a good decision. To begin with, it is prudent to write job descriptions in some detail. Subsequently, in soliciting candidates and interviewing them, it is important to ensure equal opportunity and to avoid using or appearing to use illegal criteria in making decisions. In addition, you may want to take proactive steps to recruit a diverse pool of candidates.

You should ensure that screening devices such as testing and background investigations properly reflect the requirements of the open position, that they are fair and nondiscriminatory, and that they respect individuals' privacy rights. Although you should not automatically rule out a candidate because of past problems, even a felony conviction, you do need to be reasonably sure that the individual does not pose a risk to customers, suppliers, or other employees.

In making a formal offer of employment, it is important to remember the principles of employment-at-will from Chapter One. Certainly you may make any commitments regarding length of employment, future compensation, and so forth that are appropriate for the open position, but remember that your promises, whether oral or in writing, may be enforceable. In addition, the beginning of employment is the time to make the company's employment-at-will policy clear and to address contractual provisions such as arbitration, noncompetition, and trade secret agreements.

In sum, conscientiously complying with the law imposes a certain amount of discipline on hiring and promotion processes. Many of the incentives established by the law, however, also support sound business objectives. They encourage equal treatment of individuals in a broad candidate pool, encourage managers to fully understand the candidates' credentials and background, and help ensure that both the employee and the manager understand the terms of the job offer. From the broader managerial perspective, then, legal standards are not a hindrance to good management. Instead, they should assist you in selecting the best possible individual for an open position.

Evaluating
Employees

A gain today Anne came to work only to find the stack of blank employee appraisal forms sitting reproachfully on her desk. It is true that Anne has been busy with the regular functions of her department. But she also has to admit that she has been avoiding the appraisals because they are one of the aspects of her job that she likes least.

In her mind, Anne runs through her employees. There is Jared, who is a single father with primary responsibility for two young children. His skills are terrific, but he sometimes uses some of the company's family-friendly policies such as flex time and Family Medical Leave Act leave when the children are ill or need him at home or school. Corrine is the newest employee. Her analytical abilities do not seem to measure up to her résumé, but she is enthusiastic. She is new to the area, not romantically involved, and is child-free, so she has few outside commitments. She is always willing to take on a new assignment or a task no one else wants. Jennifer, well, Jennifer is just there. She does her job, more or less. She is the only Muslim in the department, but that does not seem to have any bearing on her performance, or lack of performance. Last is Tom, the department clerk. Tom and Anne have had personality clashes since Anne took over the department about a year ago. Although Tom seems to avoid as much work as possible these days, all his prior performance evaluations were excellent.

Anne decides to avoid the performance appraisals a bit longer. As she sorts through the stack of memos and notes on her desk, she comes to some unreturned telephone messages. There she finds a message from someone calling for a reference on Javier, who retired three months ago. He had been a good performer and was the stabilizing force of the department. Anne has missed his sage counsel and hard work. The message slip reminds her that she recently heard Javier lost money in the stock market downturn and might be looking for another job.

In this chapter I address legal issues that managers like Anne need to take into account when evaluating their employees. One broad subset of issues concerns performance evaluations of current employees. The first part of this chapter discusses these issues.

I view evaluations somewhat differently from the way many people do because I believe that similar issues are involved in evaluating both current and former employees. Thus, a second subset of evaluation issues concerns references for former employees, like Javier. The interaction between company policies and the legal standards in this area is particularly interesting. Even if your company policy forbids you from providing former employees with references, you should read that section of the chapter. You are likely to find it both informative and useful.

■ Fact or Fallacy? ■

---

1. Male employees are as entitled as female employees to use their company's family-friendly programs. ☐ Fact ☐ Fallacy

2. A negative job evaluation can be sufficient evidence of unlawful discrimination for a member of a protected group to bring a lawsuit on that basis alone. ☐ Fact ☐ Fallacy

3. One safe way to avoid problems with an employee who might allege workplace discrimination is by not giving that individual any negative feedback. ☐ Fact ☐ Fallacy

4. Forced ranking systems are inherently discriminatory because not all departments have equal proportions of high and low achievers. ☐ Fact ☐ Fallacy

5. If you are having a difficult time working through the performance evaluations of your department, you can safely use your manager as a sounding board. ☐ Fact ☐ Fallacy

---

■ Legal Issues with Performance Evaluations

Companies have considerable discretion in determining what type of performance evaluation program to adopt. Of course, there are a number of important management considerations in designing such a program, including who should be involved in the evaluation process, the frequency of evaluations, the amount of input the employee being evaluated should have, and the measures to be used. Here, though, I will focus on potential legal issues that apply to any performance evaluation system.

No federal or state law requires companies to adopt any particular type of performance evaluation program or to have an appraisal program at all. Instead, some of the legal concepts I have already discussed in Chapters One and Two apply in this context. Legal challenges to performance evaluation systems are often based on claims of discrimination, negligence, or defamation. The most frequent of these claims is probably discrimination. I will discuss those types of lawsuits in the most detail because some of the concepts are not intuitive. I will close this section with negligence and defamation claims, two legal theories I have not yet discussed in this book.

Before proceeding to those issues, let me note the utility of having detailed job descriptions when the time comes to do performance reviews. In Chapter Two, I discussed reasons why accurate and careful job descriptions can be useful to managers in making hiring and promotion decisions. Job descriptions also can be of value to you in the evaluation process. They provide a point of reference for job expectations. Because job descriptions tend to be written or updated on different timetables from evaluations and typically are not explicitly part of evaluation programs, their content is often removed from the personal issues that permeate the appraisal process.

Discrimination Claims

One of the biggest challenges for Anne as she evaluates her staff is to treat each person equally. Jared, Corrine, Jennifer, and Tom all have very different talents, backgrounds, and personal lives. Apart from wanting to be fair and judicious in evaluating their performance, Anne must keep in mind that the same federal, state, and local legal standards that forbid discrimination based on protected criteria also apply in the context of performance evaluations. That means that she cannot treat one employee less favorably than another based on gender, age, or any other protected criterion.

A rather well-known case, ultimately addressed by the U.S. Supreme Court, illustrates some of the discrimination pitfalls for managers in evaluating employee performance. The controversy began when, for two years in a row, Ann Hopkins's local office submitted her name for promotion to partner status at Price

Waterhouse. During 1982, when Ann was first nominated for partnership, only 7 of the firm's 662 partners were women. Unlike any of the other candidates up for partnership, Ann had played a key role in Price Waterhouse's attainment of a $25 million consulting contract. Yet Price Waterhouse declined to elect Ann to partner status.

After being denied partnership, Ann sued Price Waterhouse, alleging gender bias in the partnership evaluation process. One of the senior members of the firm had advised Ann after the first unsuccessful nomination that she should "walk more femininely, talk more femininely, dress more femininely, wear make-up, have her hair styled, and wear jewelry."[1] Other comments in the partnership evaluations recommended she take "a course at charm school" and described her as "macho."[2] In her book about the case, Ann talks repeatedly about the novelty of riding her motorcycle to work at a very traditional firm.[3]

At her trial, Price Waterhouse clients testified on Ann's behalf, and the trial judge concluded that Ann "had no difficulty dealing with clients and her clients appear to have been very pleased with her work."[4] Moreover, Ann's expert witness testified that Price Waterhouse had engaged in sex stereotyping. In short, had Ann been a male, her aggressiveness and brusqueness probably would have worked in her favor. Price Waterhouse failed to convince the courts that it had based its denial of partnership on nondiscriminatory reasons. The court therefore ordered Price Waterhouse to return Ann Hopkins to work as a partner, with $371,000 in back pay.

The Hopkins case is a reminder that managers must be careful not to let their biases and preconceptions affect the way they evaluate employees. For example, in the opening scenario, Anne may find it unusual that Jared has so much childcare responsibility. But if the company has family-friendly policies in place and encourages flexibility in schedules to accommodate situations such as these, then it is a fact that Anne must give

Jared the same leeway under those policies that she would accord the mother of young children (Fact or Fallacy? item 1). In other words, she needs to guard against a bias that could lead to discrimination based on gender. The media is rife with stories about fathers who feel that their careers would be at risk if they took the same advantage of family-friendly policies as their female colleagues. The stories are one example of the failure of companies to ensure equal treatment of employees regardless of gender or other protected criteria. Similarly, it may be difficult to compare Corrine and Jared, given their very different skills and circumstances.

In this area, as in others, managers sometimes regard legal requirements and pitfalls as a hassle rather than an opportunity. They may feel that they have to be extra-scrupulous not to tread on the toes of someone who might conceivably bring a discrimination claim. The point here is not that you should bend over backward to avoid problems with an employee because of race, gender, or any other protected characteristic. Rather, the positive point is that you should strive to be as consistent, objective, and evenhanded as possible in your evaluations. This is not only good practice legally speaking, it is good management as well.

The trouble is that by their nature our biases often operate below the level of conscious awareness. Consequently, as a manager you need to do some self-examination as you prepare performance reviews. Put several reviews side by side. Are you comparing employees on consistent grounds? Are you communicating your concerns and praise similarly to different employees? Do you notice any patterns in your evaluations that might reflect an unconscious bias based on gender, race, religion, or age? Such a bias may show up, not because you are prejudiced, but simply because you are most comfortable with people who are similar to you.

A couple of practical tips can help here. First, after composing a performance review (whether in your mind or, as I recommend, in written form), examine the way you are phrasing your evaluation. It's often natural for managers to express performance evaluations in "I/you" language. ("*I'm* disappointed that *you* don't seem to be working as efficiently this quarter as in the past.") Sometimes, in fact, there is so much "I" in a performance evaluation that the subject of the evaluation seems to be the manager more than the employee. In any case, the effect of I/you language is to make the evaluation seem to be more about the people involved than about the employee's *performance.*

Instead, try editing out most "I's" and "you's." Rephrase the feedback in terms of performance and behavior rather than commenting on the individual as a person, and use objective criteria as the basis of your feedback. Thus you might write, "The weekly reports show some drop-off compared to last quarter in terms of the time tasks are taking to complete."

Phrasing your evaluation in terms of the performance instead of the person has several advantages. First, it avoids personalizing the feedback in a way that invites defensiveness on the part of the employee. Evaluation that comes across as a personal attack ("you aren't as efficient as you should be") is much harder to respond to constructively than well-considered observations about objective performance. Second, it focuses the employee's attention where it belongs—on the employee's performance, not on you or your opinions. It may even encourage the employee to join with you in assessing that performance. In this case, your observation may open the door to some dialogue about what happened to cause the apparent decline in efficiency. Third, concentrating on objective performance and behavior will help you achieve consistency in your evaluations of different employees. As I noted earlier, having a detailed job description can help you maintain this focus.

A second tip is simply to set a performance evaluation aside and sleep on it before you present it to the employee. Then read it, not from your own perspective as the manager—which is how you composed it—but from the employee's point of view. Try to imagine that this is your own performance review. Ask yourself how you would respond to it if your manager handed it to you. Even if it is critical, does it seem objective, balanced, and fair? If this were your own performance review, would you have any reason to question whether it is consistent with the evaluations other people receive? Apart from giving you the chance to switch perspectives, being sure to sleep on a performance evaluation also helps you to avoid the consequences of composing the evaluation at a moment when you happen to be particularly upset or under stress and say things you would regret in a calmer moment. Measures like these are not only good practice but will help you avoid legal problems that arise from not taking sufficient care with evaluations.

Even when you take care with performance evaluations, you may be concerned about giving a negative evaluation to someone who conceivably could raise a discrimination claim. Is it a fallacy that a single poor performance evaluation could be sufficient grounds for a lawsuit alleging discrimination (Fact or Fallacy? item 2)? In recent cases, courts have differed on this question. One court said that, even if the poor evaluation was based on discriminatory criteria, it would need to have some specific negative consequences in order to violate the law. Unless the employee could prove that the appraisal affected something tangible such as salary or job opportunity, then the poor evaluation was simply too insignificant to be the basis for a legal claim. In contrast, another court decided that it was likely that "an unfavorable employee assessment, placed in a personnel file to be reviewed in connection with future decisions concerning pay and promotion, could both prejudice the employee's supervisors and materially diminish his chances for advancement."[5] Therefore, the court said one negative appraisal would violate the law if the appraisal was discriminatory.

The mere possibility of a lawsuit, though, should not discourage you from giving an employee a negative performance appraisal, so long as it is based on appropriate and nondiscriminatory grounds. The typical manager accepts some risk in making business-related decisions. A negative performance appraisal can bring about a variety of positive results. In the best case, employees may be encouraged to improve their performance, and department morale may improve as hardworking employees see that you are serious about enforcing high standards and recognizing superior performance. At the very least you may be establishing the necessary documentation to ultimately terminate an underperforming employee. Instead of avoiding the difficult task of giving negative feedback because it might lead to a lawsuit, you should focus on documenting nondiscriminatory reasons for a negative performance appraisal.

Employers do win cases where the manager has kept careful records to support a poor appraisal even when that appraisal ultimately led to the termination of the employee. For example, in a recent case, State Farm Mutual Automobile Insurance Company fired Frank Wilcox, who was fifty-seven years old and had worked there for more than twenty-nine years. His supervisor had repeatedly warned Frank not to put his personal opinions in claims files. Numerous customers had complained about his rude attitude. There were no patterns of repeated complaints about any other employees. After continued poor performance, State Farm placed Frank on probationary status and fired him when he failed to improve his performance. Frank sued, alleging age discrimination. The court dismissed his case because State Farm had plenty of evidence to show that it gave Frank the poor evaluation and dismissed him because of his ongoing attitude problems and failure to follow his supervisor's directions and not because of his age.[6]

Despite cases like this one, some managers operate under the belief that it is safer to give a positive performance appraisal, or at least not to give a negative appraisal, to an employee who might sue for discrimination if the manager were to give an honest but poor appraisal (Fact or Fallacy? item 3). That approach, however, raises a host of problems. First, the manager is stuck with a poorly performing employee and few options in encouraging the employee to improve. As other employees see that the employee does not suffer any negative consequences, department morale may suffer. What may surprise the manager most, though, is that this approach does not necessarily immunize the company from a lawsuit by the poorly performing employee alleging unlawful discrimination.

Consider the case of Emma Vaughn, an African American attorney who worked as a contract analyst at Texaco. For a number of years she received regular promotions and was the highest-ranked contract analyst in the department. On the day Emma returned from a second maternity leave, her manager, Robert Edel, spoke to her about her performance. Emma then went to his manager, Roger Keller. According to Roger's note to the file, he explained to Emma that he had been told her productivity "was very low" and he "had been aware for some time of the excessive visiting by predominately blacks in her office behind closed doors." The memo went on to say that Roger advised Emma that "she was allowing herself to become a black matriarch within Texaco" and that was "preventing her from doing her primary work for the company and that it must stop."[7]

Roger found out that, after the conversation, Emma went to a friend in Texaco's legal department and told the friend that she thought Roger was prejudiced. Roger then told Robert, Emma's supervisor, not to get into any confrontations with Emma. Roger later said that "for several years he had intentionally overstated on Vaughn's annual evaluations his satisfaction with her performance because he did not have the time to spend going through procedures which would result from a lower rating and which could lead to termination." The annual evaluations showed her work to be "satisfactory."

When Texaco let Emma go (as one of the lowest-performing analysts) in a cost reduction program, she sued, alleging race discrimination. Her claim was that if she had received counseling or been put on an improvement program, as had happened with a white colleague, she would have been able to correct her shortcomings and would not have been dismissed. The court agreed that, although the managers acted in their own interest rather than due to racial hostility, Emma raised a legitimate claim of race discrimination, since she had been treated differently because of her race.[8] This is a case where the managers might have protected themselves and their company by giving Emma more negative evaluations. Also, Emma might have become a more productive employee.

In sum, the possibility of a discrimination suit resulting from a negative performance evaluation, or even from the failure to give a negative evaluation, is a reality. By their very nature, performance evaluations tend to engage an employee's defense mechanisms. Few of us enjoy being criticized. And even low-performing employees may derive a great deal of their self-worth from their work. One way for employees who are not realistic about their own job performance to rationalize their managers' criticisms with their own views is to believe the managers' analysis is based on illegal criteria. To use the opening scenario as an example, if Anne criticizes Jennifer's poor performance, Jennifer may feel she is being evaluated differently because Anne dislikes Muslims. There is no way for Anne to completely forestall this type of assumption or to be 100 percent sure Jennifer will not sue. Anne can, however, minimize these possibilities. She can carefully document her dissatisfaction with Jennifer's performance in the most objective and quantifiable way possible. Anne can present her concerns to Jennifer in a professional and respectful manner, focusing as objectively as possible on Jennifer's performance, along with suggestions for improvement. And even if she ultimately disagrees with Jennifer's responses, Anne can listen carefully to them and be prepared to reconsider the accuracy of her assessment in light of any evidence Jennifer can present.

Finally, it is important for managers to understand that disparate impact discrimination, which I discussed in the last chapter, also applies to performance evaluation systems. This is the theory of liability that caused problems for Ford Motor Company when Ford recently implemented a forced ranking system. During its first year of use, Ford's system required managers to assign their employees "grades" of A, B, or C. At least 10 percent of all employees had to receive the grade of C. Ford later lowered that requirement to 5 percent. Receiving a grade of C could result in a loss of raises and bonuses. Two consecutive Cs could result in an employee's termination. Groups of older white males sued, alleging that Ford used the forced ranking system to try to increase diversity so that a disproportionate number of older white males received grades of C. Ford eventually eliminated the requirement that a fixed percentage of employees receive Cs and settled two of the class action lawsuits for $10.5 million.[9]

The issue here is not the forced ranking system in and of itself. Contrary to Fact or Fallacy? item 4, such a system does not inherently leave a company open to discrimination complaints. In fact, General Electric has successfully used a similar system for a number of years. Other companies have copied GE's system, which many people think is an important factor in GE's success. The general principle is that *any* performance evaluation system constitutes illegal discrimination if it is used to discriminate against any person or group of people based on prohibited criteria. More to the point in the case of Ford, any system that has the effect of assigning low rankings at significantly disproportionate rates to members of a protected group raises the potential of a claim of disparate impact discrimination.

Although the potential of discrimination complaints is the main legal hazard associated with performance reviews, two other issues deserve mention, negligence and defamation. I'll briefly address each.

Negligence Claims

There is a slender possibility that an unhappy employee could sue for negligence in the way a manager has prepared performance evaluations. Negligence is a general legal concept that typically applies where one person or company owes a duty to act reasonably but, instead, acts in an unreasonable way that causes injury. For example, a retail store owes a duty to its customers to provide a reasonably safe environment. Imagine a situation where an employee mops the floor but does not put out a "wet floor" sign. If a customer slips on the wet floor, the store probably would be liable because its employee's actions were not reasonable.

While negligence is a familiar concept to most people, you might be surprised to learn that a few courts over the years have permitted employees to bring negligence claims based on performance evaluations. The following case, though, shows how unlikely it is that this type of claim will be successful.

Darwin Ferrett worked as a test driver for General Motors for thirteen years. Because of Darwin's excessive absenteeism, his supervisor twice put him on Performance Improvement Plans that required him to improve his attendance or be fired. After Darwin successfully completed both Improvement Plans, he again started missing work. His supervisor reminded Darwin of the attendance problems but did not put him on a third Performance Improvement Plan or tell him that he was likely to be fired. A week later General Motors terminated Darwin's employment.

Darwin sued, alleging that the supervisor had been negligent in evaluating Darwin's situation and failing to put him on a third Performance Improvement Plan. The court rejected Darwin's claims. It made clear that the law does not require employers to perform evaluations or to correctly perform evaluations they voluntarily undertake of at-will employees.[10]

More generally, so long as your employees are employees-at-will and you avoid discriminating against people based on protected criteria, the legal standards are deferential to your rights to evaluate your employees as you see fit. Courts recognize that negligent evaluation claims tend to be inconsistent with an employer's right to terminate an at-will employee for any reason, even an arbitrary or capricious reason, so long as it is not an illegal reason.

Defamation

Finally, employees sometimes file lawsuits claiming that their performance appraisals are defamatory. Legally speaking, a defamation claim requires three elements: (1) a false statement of fact that (2) is "published," meaning communicated to someone other than the plaintiff, either negligently or with malice, and that (3) causes damage to the plaintiff's reputation. You may have heard the terms libel and slander. *Libel* is defamation based on written statements whereas *slander* is defamation based on verbal statements. The legal theory of defamation might apply to performance evaluations that contain factual misstatements, are communicated to people other than the employee, and damage the employee's reputation.

In this context, though, state law sometimes provides protection for employers. In a recent New York case, Areta Brattis received a negative performance appraisal from Dennis Farrell, the senior vice president of finance at Fox/Liberty Networks. The appraisal conveyed the supervisor's "general impression that you are not getting all aspects of the Business mjrs [managers] job done satisfactorily"[11] and similar statements. Farrell then shared the appraisal with Brattis's new supervisor, human resources, and other company employees. Brattis sued for defamation.

The New York court dismissed the lawsuit before trial. First, it agreed with the company that the statements in the appraisal were protected opinion. Only false statements of fact can provide the basis for a defamation suit. In contrast, each of us is entitled to express our own honestly held opinion, even if that opinion is derogatory of someone else. In the words of the court: "Under New York law, the evaluation of an employee's performance, even an unsatisfactory evaluation, is a matter of opinion that cannot be objectively categorized as true or false and cannot be actionable."[12] A statement of fact, however, does not become protected simply by adding the phrase "in my opinion." If, for example, someone says "In my opinion Jane is a thief," some courts may decide that whether or not Jane is a thief is a matter of fact. The statement, then, can be the basis of a defamation lawsuit. Second, the court determined that even if the evaluation had included some false statements of fact, the evaluation would have constituted a privileged communication. Generally, if someone has a duty to make a statement, then that statement is protected even if it contains a false statement of fact. Employers have a need to evaluate employees, to preserve evaluations, and to communicate the results of the evaluations to certain individuals. Again, the words of the court are clear: "New York courts have not been hesitant to invoke qualified privilege to protect an employer's statements made in an employment context."[13]

In sum, it is theoretically possible but difficult for employees to win claims based on the idea that their manager defamed them in a performance appraisal. Still, the possibility of such a claim is a reason for caution in discussing or circulating performance evaluations (Fact or Fallacy? item 5). If Anne, for example, decides to discuss the appraisals of her staff with people who do not need to know that information, she may risk losing her qualified privilege. Or say she talks about those appraisals while at lunch with her manager at a local restaurant. She brings up the topic because she is having trouble preparing the appraisals and wants her manager's advice. That seems like a reasonable communication with someone who is entitled to know the results of the evaluation and is appropriate for Anne to consult for assistance. But in her fury over Tom's latest snide remark,

Anne may carelessly misstate some important facts about Tom's performance and be overheard by others who know Tom. In this case, Anne may be guilty of defaming Tom by negligently talking about him and conveying false facts where others who have no right to that information can hear her. This is not only legally risky but poor management practice as well. The most prudent course for managers is to treat performance evaluations as sensitive and confidential, and to discuss them only in private with those who have a genuine need to know.

■ Process Issues and Long-Term Use of Performance Evaluations

The legal issues I have discussed so far relate primarily to the content of performance appraisals. There are also some other concerns for managers relating to the process for conducting evaluations and their long-term use.

With respect to the process for evaluations, many employers permit employees to obtain a copy of their performance appraisals. In some states, such as Michigan, state law gives employees a right to those copies. Legal requirements aside, this type of policy also tends to make good management sense. Performance feedback sessions can be stressful, and an employee may not absorb everything that you, as manager, are trying to communicate. Providing the employee with a copy of the written evaluation can help reinforce and clarify your concerns. It can also help prevent misunderstandings that arise because an employee does not correctly interpret your oral feedback or because you may not have expressed your feedback as thoughtfully or carefully as you would in writing.

For similar reasons, numerous companies require employees to sign their performance evaluations. That approach makes it very difficult for employees to later claim their manager never provided any performance feedback or showed them an appraisal. Sometimes employees have the explicit right to attach statements to appraisals if they disagree with the evaluation. Other companies have informal policies that permit employees to take a variety of actions, such as appealing to a higher level of management, in response to appraisals they perceive as problematic. Although appeals or employee statements can create concerns for the manager who did the original appraisal, these programs do have the advantage of surfacing problems so they can be dealt with and adding credibility to appraisal programs.

Managers should also remember that performance evaluations can have long-term implications. As I have already noted, a failure to document reasons for dissatisfaction with an employee's performance could work to the company's detriment in the case of a discrimination complaint. More generally, if Anne fails to confront and document performance issues during the appraisal process, she could have a difficult time firing an employee later, when she finally gets fed up with substandard performance. Similarly, inadequate appraisals may constrain her decision making if the company mandates a downsizing at some point in the future. It is not uncommon for companies to make layoff decisions based at least in part on the content of performance evaluations.

■ Evaluation of Former Employees

At the beginning of this chapter, I mentioned my belief that the concept of evaluation also applies to former employees. The primary way in which managers have to deal with this is through attempts by others to check references given by employees who worked for the manager. In this section, I discuss the legal considerations of providing references as well as a few more general points about good practice in this area.

■ Fact or Fallacy? ■

---

1. State law discourages employers from providing references for former employees because it makes employers liable for bad references.   □ Fact   □ Fallacy

2. Even if managers typically do not give references for former employees, there is no legal risk in making an exception in order to give a positive reference for an outstanding achiever.   □ Fact   □ Fallacy

3. One legally safe way to negotiate an employee's departure is to offer the employee a positive appraisal if the employee will agree to resign.   □ Fact   □ Fallacy

4. Giving a former employee a verbal reference is not necessarily any safer legally than providing a written reference.   □ Fact   □ Fallacy

5. If someone calls you asking for a reference on one of your former employees, that person is considering your former employee for employment.   □ Fact   □ Fallacy

---

Defamation and References

Earlier in this chapter I discussed defamation as it applies to performance evaluations. Once you understand the concept of defamation, it is easy to see how it might apply to references for former employees. Assume that Anne receives a telephone call from a manager at another company who is considering hiring Javier. Assume also that Anne, either negligently or with malice, makes a false statement of fact about Javier's performance that hurts his chances of getting the job. Would Javier have a valid defamation claim against Anne?

In past decades, Javier would have such a claim. One expert in this area cites research indicating that in the 1980s it was not unusual for plaintiffs to win million-dollar verdicts in these kinds of cases.[14] It was to minimize such legal liability that numerous employers instituted policies prohibiting managers from providing any detailed references for former employees. Such policies continue to be in force today. The vast majority of managers in my executive education classes tell me that they are forbidden to provide more than the most basic information in response to reference requests, such as dates of employment and perhaps job title.

From a narrow perspective, such policies are a rational response by employers. After all, Anne's company gains nothing by providing an honest reference for Javier. On the negative side, it would take some of Anne's time to respond carefully and thoroughly, and by providing a reference, the company would accept some legal risk.

Moreover, companies face no threat of legal liability by simply declining to provide a reference, even regarding an individual whom the employer knows to be dangerous. I have never seen a case lost by an employer who consistently declined to give references. For example, when Jeffrey St. Clair worked at St. Joseph Nursing Home, before being fired he was warned twenty-four times for being violent and using drugs and alcohol. Subsequently, Maintenance Management Corporation hired Jeffrey. Jeffrey then savagely beat and murdered Clyde A. Moore Sr., a security guard at a facility where Maintenance Management had assigned Jeffrey to work. In its decision that St. Joseph Nursing Home had no duty to provide Maintenance Management with information about Jeffrey's dangerous tendencies, the court said: "We conclude that a former employer has no duty to disclose malefic information about a former employee to the former employee's prospective employer."[15]

This is one circumstance, however, where the narrow perspective does not reflect the long-term best interest of employers as a whole. Without question, prior job performance tends to be a valuable indicator for companies screening job applicants. If employers could honestly share information about former employees, employers as a community could make better hiring decisions and would be better off. Similarly, good employees would be better off if their former employers would be willing to provide accurate employment references.

During the last ten years, states have recognized that the legal system was discouraging employers from providing references. As a result, a majority of states have passed laws attempting to change the status quo. The methods varied by state, but the new laws tend to have some common factors. The statutes typically utilize a concept of privilege similar to the one I described for job evaluations. So long as the manager is acting in good faith in providing a job reference, even an inaccurate statement of fact that damages the reputation of the former employee does not provide the basis for a legal claim. The state laws do vary in their details, however. For example, some states revoke the employer's privilege if the manager discloses certain types of confidential information about the former employee. In general, however, contrary to Fact or Fallacy? item 1, state law does not discourage employers from providing references for former employees.

Changes in the law have not been successful in encouraging employers to share more information. The majority of companies continue to prohibit managers and human resources departments from providing anything other than the most basic facts on former employees. In my view, this is unfortunate, because the restrictions on references work against the common best interest of employers.

Other Legal Hazards

My informal surveys of managers tell me something else too: most managers will occasionally violate their company's policy and provide a job reference for a particularly well-deserving former employee, in the belief that they run no legal risk in doing so (Fact or Fallacy? item 2). Before you decide that you would never violate your company's policy, consider another situation involving Anne. Suppose she receives a call from Javier, that terrific former employee who retired a few months ago. Javier has lost a great deal of money in the recent stock market downturn and is desperately looking for another job. Anne regretfully explains that the company's financial performance has been soft and, at least until it turns around, there will not be any opportunities there for Javier. He tells Anne that he understands but he has been having some trouble convincing potential employers that he has the energy and current skills necessary for the available job openings. He knows that age discrimination is illegal, but he suspects that his age is not an advantage in the job market. Javier asks Anne if she would be willing to speak on his behalf to potential employers.

Javier really needs a job, and to get one he needs Anne's help. Anne knows that he was a capable and dedicated employee. If you were in Anne's situation, are you sure you would refuse to help Javier? What if you received a call from a good friend at another company who was considering hiring Javier? And if you agreed to help either Javier or your friend, would you be running any legal risk?

One consideration in evaluating potential legal risk involves a principle that should be becoming obvious at this point: managers should treat employees, including former employees, consistently. If Anne treats Javier differently from other former employees, she may face a claim of unlawful discrimination. Although she had no discriminatory intention, former employees who received equivalent raises and performance evaluations but were denied references (consistent with company policy) might charge discrimination based on a protected category such as national origin or gender. It is also possible that an individual who does not receive a recommendation might sue for defamation because the implication is that he was a poor performer. These risks, though, may be ones that Anne is prepared to accept.

In some instances, managers are tempted to make another type of exception, encouraging a problem employee to resign by promising the person a favorable letter of reference (Fact or Fallacy? item 3). This scenario, too, can carry some legal risk. According to news reports, Allstate Insurance Co. offered Paul Calden a good letter of reference and severance pay in return for his resignation. Reportedly, Allstate knew that Calden had "brought a pistol to work, made threats against co-workers and engaged in bizarre behavior in the workplace, such as performing devil worship and stating that he was an alien from outer space."[16] Calden used Allstate's reference letter to obtain a job at Fireman's Fund. He later shot five fellow employees at Fireman's Fund before killing himself. Allstate settled the lawsuits brought by families of the victims, so it is unclear whether Allstate would have been held legally accountable for the letter of reference. But prudence, not to mention concern for the risk an employee might pose to others, suggests that most managers would do well to avoid giving a letter of reference under these circumstances.

In another case, this one in California, a court clearly decided that individuals who provided a positive letter of reference and their employers could be held liable for writing an alarmingly inaccurate letter. Randi W., a thirteen-year-old student who was not fully named because she was a minor, alleged that Robert Gadams, vice principal of her school, sexually assaulted her in his office. The school had hired Gadams, at least in part, in reliance upon letters of reference written by individuals at four school districts that had previously employed him. Those letters made statements such as "I wouldn't hesitate to recommend Mr. Gadams for any position!" and I "would recommend him for almost any administrative position he wishes to pursue." One described him as "an upbeat, enthusiastic administrator who relates well to the students."[17]

Mr. Gadams had left each of those districts after engaging in inappropriate sexually related conduct with students. The court decided that former employers and managers who provide letters of recommendation may be liable for harm caused at a subsequent employer if the letter "amounts to an affirmative misrepresentation presenting a foreseeable and substantial risk of physical harm to a third person."[18] That is a narrow legal standard that poses no risk to a manager who provides a letter of reference to a former employee whose work at a subsequent employer does not meet the employer's expectations. But it does pose a risk to managers who provide references for former employees they know to be violent or otherwise dangerous.

At times managers use one of two techniques in an attempt to avoid breaking their company's policy against providing references or to decrease the possibility of liability. Sometimes a manager will provide a former employee with a personal letter of reference. Such a personal letter of reference can be appropriate and avoid violating company policy, provided the manager does know the individual well on a personal basis, never addresses the individual's work history, writes on personal stationery, and does not mention being the individual's former manager. Those types of letters are rare, though, and they tend to be far less valuable to a job candidate than a letter discussing the person's work history.

The second tactic some managers use is to provide oral, but not written, references. For example, they are willing to provide a reference to a potential employer who telephones them, but will not write a letter that could be used as evidence against them in case of a lawsuit. As suggested by Fact or Fallacy? item 4, this approach is not necessarily safer than refusing to commit a reference to writing. One problem is that it becomes the manager's word against the other party's as to what was said during the phone call. That may require any subsequent lawsuit to go all the way through trial so a fact finder can decide whose testimony is most credible. A written document would not be subject to that type of dispute. Also, many people are more likely to be careful and accurate when writing a letter than when engaging in a telephone conversation. A good questioner may lead you to verbalize things about a former employee that you would never put in writing. And if you are not willing to say it in writing, you probably should not be saying it aloud either.

That leads to a final concern with providing references. It is a fallacy to assume that the person who is contacting you about a former employee is a potential employer (Fact or Fallacy? item 5). Numerous reference checking services advertise their services to individuals who want to know what a former manager would say about them. A story in the *Wall Street Journal* described these services and told of Jana Lynn Tudor's situation. She had trouble finding a new position as a pediatric nurse and suspected her prior employer might be giving her a poor employment reference. To find out whether her suspicions were justified, Tudor hired a company to check. For a fee, the company called her former manager and prepared a contemporaneous transcript of the telephone call. Tudor used the transcript to sue her former employer for providing "false and derogatory information" about her.[19] According to the story, a jury awarded her $1.6 million in damages. The moral here is to be circumspect when you provide references and to verify the identity of the person requesting a reference.

CHAPTER SUMMARY

Many if not most managers share Anne's dislike for performance evaluations. But, done well, performance appraisals can help motivate your staff, can keep your group working at a high level, and can be used as a way to justify terminating chronic low-performers. Done poorly, performance appraisals can result in legal liability.

As is so often true in employment issues, the most important concept to remember in doing evaluations is to treat employees as fairly and equally as possible. That means using the same standards for all employees in the same position instead of using criteria that might be gender-biased or otherwise dependent upon illegal considerations. It also means providing honest feedback and counseling, even if that feedback is negative. For the reasons discussed in the chapter, I believe it is prudent on both legal and managerial grounds to put performance evaluations in writing. In addition, specific state laws may affect the procedural requirements of the appraisal process, such as the right of employees to obtain copies of their evaluations.

Similar considerations apply to evaluations of former employees. In addition, laws in the majority of states now provide some protection for those who give references for former employees, and doing so would seem to be in the common interest of employers. Nevertheless, most employers still maintain policies that prohibit managers and human resources departments from providing anything other than basic employment data in a reference check.

In exceptional circumstances, many managers will provide an especially deserving employee with a favorable employment recommendation, but doing so carries some legal risks, particularly the possibility of a discrimination complaint from another former employee.

It can be unwise to provide a positive reference for an employee in return for the person's resignation. If you do provide any former employee with a recommendation, it should be accurate. In particular, you should never provide a positive recommendation for someone you know poses a risk of harm to others. Finally, it is best to put references in writing and to be sure you know the identity of the person who is asking for the letter.

Avoiding Discrimination

Choon Lee, who manages a fifteen-person sales staff, has two human resources issues on his mind. First, the company is beginning an effort to enhance the skills of its workforce by sending some of its people to an executive education program at a major university, and Choon has been asked to choose one of his people to attend. Choon knows that selection for the program is seen as a signal of high potential within the company. He expects that a number of his staff would like to attend. Choon isn't looking forward to making his selection, since he knows that whatever choice he makes will disappoint several other people. As he ponders his decision, however, a possible discrimination complaint is the furthest thing from his mind.

Second, Choon just received a memorandum about a new internal training program. The plan is to train every employee regarding the company's Nondiscrimination and Antiharassment Policy. Choon will be going through the program first, but eventually each member of his staff will attend. Choon questions whether it makes sense for the company to spend so much time and money on this training. Choon did recently hear a rumor that the manager of another department, Jim, had fired one of the engineers in the department, Kimdra, after she refused to sleep with him. But no one in Choon's own department has ever complained about discrimination or harassment. If there is a problem with a particular manager, Choon wonders, why not deal with just the offender? Or, at most, couldn't the company limit the training to managers instead of disrupting the workflow by putting everyone through it?

I find that most managers, like Choon, have a good understanding of many of the basic concepts in nondiscrimination law. This is also an area, however, where managers' understanding is often incomplete and fallacies abound. Choon, for example, is very attentive to discrimination issues in hiring and promotions, but he doesn't think of discrimination as a potential issue when it comes to things like picking the most suitable candidate for a training program. Similarly, he sees harassment as a problem only in relation to managers' behavior toward employees, so he questions why his entire staff should go through an antiharassment program.

In this chapter, I address basic principles all managers should know about discrimination laws and harassment. Obviously, I cannot address all the relevant issues in detail. The law in this area is so complex that most law schools offer one or more courses exclusively on nondiscrimination in employment, and the textbooks for those courses are hundreds of pages long. I will, though, set out key factors in nondiscrimination law. I will discuss the characteristics that are protected, the types of employment actions that are subject to the laws, and some surprising ways in which the laws do not protect employees. I will also explain the specific defenses available to employers in those limited circumstances where it is necessary for managers to consider criteria such as gender that it typically would be illegal to consider when dealing with employees.

One question managers often ask is how an employee can prove a decision was made based on a discriminatory criterion when the manager can point to a legitimate, nondiscriminatory basis for the decision. Because of the interest in that question, I will briefly explain the method the courts have developed to try to ascertain the truth when managers and employees tell very different stories. I will also touch on the related topic of legal issues concerning diversity and affirmative action programs.

Next, I will consider the subject of employer liability in the area of harassment. Finally, I will close the chapter with a brief note on the unique issues raised by claims of religious discrimination and harassment.

■ Fact or Fallacy? ■

1. Federal law prohibits discrimination based on virtually any group characteristic including gender, race, national origin, religion, and sexual orientation. □ Fact □ Fallacy

2. There are some employers who do not need to comply with federal nondiscrimination laws. □ Fact □ Fallacy

3. Nondiscrimination laws apply to all job-related decisions, including transfers. □ Fact □ Fallacy

4. So long as the manager would have made exactly the same decision based on legal criteria such as performance, it is OK to consider otherwise illegal criteria, such as religion, as a plus or minus factor in decision making. □ Fact □ Fallacy

5. All employers must have an affirmative action plan. □ Fact □ Fallacy

■ Coverage of Nondiscrimination Laws

One of the keys to understanding the nondiscrimination laws is to know what characteristics are protected by the laws. Most managers could list at least some of the characteristics protected by Title VII, the first significant federal law prohibiting discrimination, when it was enacted in 1967. Those criteria are race, color, religion, sex, and national origin. Part of the complexity of nondiscrimination law comes in understanding what additional characteristics are protected in the state or locality where your employees work, what additional characteristics have become protected by various federal laws since 1967, and what characteristics remain unprotected.

To begin with, states and localities cannot take away protections provided by federal law to employees of nongovernmental employers. But state and local laws can be, and frequently are, more protective than federal law requires. As a result, the types of criteria managers can consider in employment decision making vary widely from place to place. To take just a few examples, Michigan prohibits discrimination based on height and weight; Alaska prohibits discrimination based on a change in marital status; Vermont prohibits discrimination based on place of birth; and Louisiana prohibits discrimination based on sickle cell traits. Moreover, since 1967, federal law has become increasingly protective of employees by adding nondiscrimination provisions for new criteria, including pregnancy, age forty and older, and disability. A statute enacted in 1994, the Uniformed Services Employment and Reemployment Rights Act (USERRA), clarifies employment protections and prohibits discrimination against existing or prospective employees based on service in the U.S. military.

Even given the breadth of the protections under nondiscrimination law, some characteristics receive little or no protection. For example, the first Fact or Fallacy? item is a fallacy because federal law does not prohibit discrimination based on sexual orientation, though a few states and a number of localities do prohibit employers from discriminating on this basis. It can be surprisingly difficult, however, to determine whether or not a particular decision or action by an employer is based on a prohibited criterion.

Consider the situation of John Bibby, a gay man, who worked at Philadelphia Coca-Cola Bottling Company. Bibby sued the company, claiming that supervisors and fellow employees harassed him and treated him differently because he was gay. As I have just noted, federal law does not prohibit discrimination based on sexual orientation. However, in 1998 the U.S. Supreme Court decided, in a case of harassment by male employees on an oil rig against another male employee, that federal law does prohibit *sexual harassment* by members of the same sex as the harassed individual. Thus in a case like Bibby's, the plaintiff would have to prove that he was discriminated against or harassed based on his sex, not because of his sexual orientation. In practice, it clearly can be difficult to distinguish between harassment based on sex (illegal) and harassment based on sexual orientation (legal). In any case, since Bibby had only claimed that he had been harassed and mistreated because of his sexual orientation, he lost his case.[1]

To further complicate matters, as I discussed in the case involving Ann Hopkins and Price Waterhouse in Chapter Three, federal law makes it illegal to discriminate based on *sexual stereotypes*. Given the context of Hopkins's situation, it is also illegal to discriminate based on departures from sexual stereotypes. Thus, in another case that eventually settled, the court decided that it would constitute harassment based on sex if a man's coworkers abused him because he wore an earring. In that case, the man was treated differently because he did not comply with gender stereotypes.

Cases that require courts to draw fine lines in determining whether employers have based decisions on prohibited criteria are by no means limited to sexual orientation. For example, in one situation a manager fired a female employee who was pregnant with his child because she refused to have an abortion. The employee sued, alleging discrimination based on gender and pregnancy, but lost her case. The court decided that the manager did not fire her because she was a woman. Nor did he fire her because she was pregnant. He had no animus toward other women, pregnant or not, and would not have fired this employee had she been pregnant with someone else's child. The bottom line for the court was that, while the manager's action may have been despicable, it was not illegal discrimination based on pregnancy or gender.

Employment discrimination laws are limited in their application in at least two other ways. First, except for USERRA, which applies to all employers, each of the federal laws applies only to employers that meet a minimum size threshold. Thus Fact or Fallacy? item 2 is true. Employers with fewer than fifteen employees are exempt from Title VII and the Americans with Disabilities Act. The federal Age Discrimination in Employment Act applies to employers with at least twenty employees. Again, state and local laws may be more protective. As an example, Michigan's basic nondiscrimination in employment law applies to employers with one or more employees.

Second, nondiscrimination laws apply only to specified actions by employers. For example, the basic provision of Title VII says: "It shall be an unlawful employer practice for an employer to fail or refuse to hire or to discharge any individual, or otherwise to discriminate against any individual with respect to his compensation, terms, conditions, or privileges of employment, because of such individual's race, color, religion, sex, or national origin. . . ."[2] In addition, a great many of the laws regulating employment, including all federal nondiscrimination laws, prohibit employers from discriminating or taking other specified negative actions against an employee who claims violation of the law or otherwise relies on its provisions. As I noted in Chapter One, employers face particularly significant liability when a judge or jury determines the employer has retaliated against an employee for pursuing the employee's legal rights.

Application of these standards, however, is not always intuitive. The question raised by both the nondiscrimination and the antiretaliation prohibitions is what actions short of firing, refusing to hire or promote, or creating inequities in compensation constitute discrimination with respect to the "terms, conditions, or privileges of employment." The most general answer is that the action probably has to be significant or material, as opposed to inconsequential or trivial. The courts, however, are in some disagreement on the exact legal analysis to be applied and how to use the analysis in various situations.

For example, consider the case of elementary school teacher Susan Sanchez, which I will simplify for purposes of illustration. A former nun, Sanchez had taught in Catholic schools for twenty-four years. She then was a principal of a Catholic school for five years before joining the Denver public school system. After approximately fourteen years, the school system transferred Sanchez to a school that was about twenty-five minutes farther from her home than the school where she taught before. Not only did the transfer significantly lengthen Sanchez's commuting time, she also found it embarrassing that she was the fourth-grade teacher who was forced to transfer instead of either of her two younger male colleagues. Sanchez alleged that she was transferred because of her gender and age.

The court decided that the transfer simply was not significant enough of a detriment to Sanchez to constitute a discriminatory act, even if the reason for the transfer was discriminatory. The court labeled the transfer as a "mere inconvenience or alteration of job responsibilities."[3] Numerous courts agree that lateral transfers, even when they are transfers to a job the worker does not want, do not constitute illegal discrimination. In one case the U.S. Postal Service reorganized, resulting in the transfer of a superintendent of station and branch operations. Because he kept his title, benefits, and so forth, the transfer was not an adverse employment action even though the new job was farther from his home than his prior position had been.[4]

Other transfers, however, have been held to constitute discrimination or retaliation. One case involved Cheryl Davis, an employee of Sioux City. After she filed a formal charge of sexual harassment, the city eliminated Davis's position and transferred her. She later sued, claiming that her transfer constituted unlawful retaliation. The city defended itself on the ground that Davis received a higher salary in the new job than she had earned in the old job. A jury, however, awarded a victory to Davis, who argued that the transfer was an adverse employment action because she no longer had supervisory duties and the new position offered less opportunity for advancement and pay increases.[5]

Similarly, a New York court decided that a transfer from "an 'elite' division . . . which provided prestige and opportunity for advancement, to a less prestigious unit with little opportunity for professional growth" would be a sufficiently negative action to constitute unlawful discrimination.[6] And, in the case of an employee that Arlington International Racecourse transferred from one facility to another after she complained of sex discrimination, the court determined that a "dramatic downward shift in skill level required to perform job responsibilities" would be sufficient to constitute an unlawful adverse employment action.[7] The employee, Dana Hoffman-Dombrowski, complained that she went from being responsible for many aspects of the staffing of hundreds of clerks to a situation encompassing five clerks and emptying lottery machines at a "small, dirty, roach infested facility so crime ridden that guards and police officers must escort her to her car in the evening."[8]

So what does this mean for the situation facing Choon Lee? Based on the size of Choon's staff, it appears that the company is large enough to be regulated by federal nondiscrimination laws. Furthermore, these laws apply to his decision on which employee to select for the coveted executive education program. A significant training opportunity that is likely to affect future decisions on promotions and compensation probably would be sufficiently material or consequential to affect the "terms, conditions, or privileges" of employment. Therefore, Choon cannot discriminate based on any of the criteria protected by federal law as he makes his decision. In addition, Choon should remember that his state or locality may prohibit discrimination on a wider variety of grounds than federal law does.

While the law on employment discrimination can be ambiguous and complex, it should encourage Choon to make his decision based on job-related criteria rather than his employees' personal characteristics. The legal standards also may encourage Choon to consider his decision more carefully than he otherwise would and to document the reasons for his selection. In total these incentives not only discourage the kinds of discrimination that our society has deemed inappropriate but may lead Choon to a better outcome than he would have achieved in the absence of the legal standards.

■ Defending Against a Charge of Discrimination

An employer faced with a charge of unlawful employment discrimination typically has three possible ways to defend itself. First, the employer might argue that the basis for the employment-related decision or action was in fact a legal basis, and not a discriminatory one. Or, depending on the context, the employer might argue one of two more technical defenses. The first defense applies in a situation where the employer admits basing a decision on criterion that typically would be illegal. However, the employer argues that, given its particular circumstances, the criterion constituted a bona fide occupational qualification (BFOQ). The second defense concerns cases in which an employee alleges disparate impact discrimination, that is, that the employer's screening criteria, while neutral on the surface, had the effect of screening out a protected group at a significantly disproportionate rate. Employers may defend against disparate impact charges by proving that the neutral screening criteria are a business necessity and no less discriminatory criteria could be used. In this section, I discuss each of these defenses.

Defense #1: We Did Not Discriminate

First, the employer might respond to a charge of discrimination by arguing that the manager who made the employment-related decision based the decision on legal criteria such as poor performance, rather than illegal criteria such as the employee's religion. Here, any corroborating evidence—contemporaneous memoranda to the file, performance evaluations, notes—may help support the manager's explanation. But if the employee has any evidence to the contrary, such as statements by the manager criticizing the employee's religious practices, then the employee may be able to proceed to trial. It may even be sufficient for the employee to show that the manager used an illegal criterion as a factor in the decision making even if the manager also considered legal criteria.

Many of these cases thus take on a "he said–she said" character, with each side presenting a very different view of the basis for the decision in question. In response, the courts have developed specific approaches in resolving these types of disputes. Understanding the courts' approaches can be useful to managers in evaluating risks, preparing documentation, and planning strategy. After discussing the remaining two types of employer defenses, I explain the analytic patterns used by the courts.

Defense #2: We Need to Discriminate

In very limited circumstances, it may be necessary to the business for a manager to make an employment-related decision based on what typically would be illegal criteria. In those situations, the federal nondiscrimination law explicitly permits employers to rely on a bona fide occupational qualification, or BFOQ, although the federal BFOQ defense is not available for decisions based on race or color. State and local nondiscrimination laws tend to contain similar BFOQ provisions. The first thing to remember, however, is that this exception is very limited, and courts are understandably skeptical of the BFOQ defense. After all, the defense essentially permits employers to discriminate based on criteria other than race and color that our society has deemed inappropriate for employment decision making. So if you make a decision intending to rely on a BFOQ, you should evaluate the circumstances carefully with a legal adviser.

There are some general situations, though, where the BFOQ defense tends to be applicable. The federal statute provides that "it shall not be an unlawful employment practice for an employer to hire and employ employees,. . . on the basis of his religion, sex, or national origin in those certain instances where religion, sex or national origin is a bona fide occupational qualification reasonably necessary to the normal operation of that particular business or enterprise."[9] Two examples of when it may be necessary to consider religion, sex, or national origin are authenticity and privacy intrusions. Authenticity issues arise when, often for credibility purposes, a job requires an employee to have particular characteristics. For example, if a male actor applied for the role of Satine in the film *Moulin Rouge*, a role actually played by Nicole Kidman, the producers probably could legally refuse to hire him because of his gender. Although employers cannot normally consider gender as a factor in making a hiring decision, in this instance it arguably is essential for credibility purposes that the role be played by a female. A real case that illustrates the concept of authenticity arose after a Wal-Mart store hired a female applicant to fill the role of Santa Claus in the store's annual Christmas program. Children would get on Santa's lap, talk about the gifts they hoped to receive for Christmas, and have their picture taken. Parents complained to store management when some children asked why Santa had breasts. Wal-Mart fired the Santa because of her gender, and the woman sued. Applying Kentucky state law, the court ruled in Wal-Mart's favor.[10] It seems that authenticity required that Santa be played by a male.

However, again, I warn that this is a limited concept. A BFOQ does not exist simply because customers may prefer an employee with certain characteristics or because the company would like to market itself in a certain way. An illustrative example of this point occurred when Southwest Airlines launched its business in the 1970s. It decided to market itself to traveling businessmen with the slogan "At last there is somebody else up there who loves you." In line with the image it was trying to promote, Southwest refused to hire males as flight attendants, and a group of males sued. Even the plaintiffs conceded that Southwest's strategy had been successful (in fact, to this day, Southwest's stock symbol is "LUV"). But, they argued, the refusal to hire male flight attendants constituted unlawful gender discrimination.

Southwest defended its policy on the grounds that having female flight attendants (who were dressed in hot pants and high boots) was a critical part of its corporate strategy. The court rejected that argument, saying: "In order not to undermine Congress' purpose to prevent employers from 'refusing to hire an individual based on stereotyped characterizations of the sexes,' a BFOQ for sex must be denied where sex is merely useful for attracting customers of the opposite sex, but where hiring both sexes will not alter or undermine the essential function of the employer's business."[11] In short, the law requires a focus on the duties of the job. The key duties of a flight attendant are to ensure passenger safety, resolve issues such as those involving seating, and provide food and beverages. The court reminded Southwest that men could perform all of those duties just as well as women could.

The concepts used in the Southwest case mean that an employer very well could lose an argument that all wait staff in a Chinese restaurant need to be of Chinese origin. The essence of the job, after all, would seem to be taking orders and delivering food and beverages to the table. It is even possible in this day of body costumes, makeup, and technology that a male actor could authentically play a female movie role.

Privacy intrusions sometimes justify a BFOQ. For example, a psychiatric hospital serving both children and teens, some of whom had been sexually abused, successfully argued that gender was a BFOQ for the position of child care specialist. The hospital was sued for taking gender into account when scheduling the specialists. The court acknowledged the reasonable necessity of having a child care specialist of the same gender perform work such as escorting a child to the bathroom and assisting with bathing. The court also recognized that providing specialists of a specific gender in therapeutic circumstances could be necessary in communicating with the children, particularly those who had suffered sexual abuse.[12]

Again, though, the circumstances in which concern over privacy intrusions justify a BFOQ are very limited. One group of weight loss clinics refused to hire males as counselors. Approximately 95 percent of the clinics' customers were women. The clinics argued that males could not perform the measurements—done with calipers and measuring tapes—of female customers without intruding on their privacy. Nor could men provide the counseling on sensitive emotional and personal issues that might affect weight loss. The court rejected these arguments, saying that any privacy invasions were minimal. Measurements were typically taken with the client fully clothed. When a client objected, the measurements simply were not taken. In short, the court determined that men can use a measuring tape and calipers as accurately as women can. They also can counsel on weight loss issues. To the extent that the clinics' overwhelmingly female client population preferred female counselors, the court made the same point as was made in the Southwest Airlines case. Customer preference does not legitimize otherwise unlawful discrimination. Although weight loss clients might prefer a counselor of the same gender, it was not necessary for the essence of the job that a counselor be of a specific gender. Therefore, the court held that gender was not a BFOQ for the position of weight loss counselor.[13]

These cases help to illustrate the difficult judgments courts must make when employers assert BFOQ exceptions—as well as the skepticism with which courts regard such claims. Before you engage in what otherwise would be intentional and illegal discrimination, you should thoroughly review your situation with legal counsel.

Defense #3: We Are Screening for Job Qualification

Just as a BFOQ is sometimes available as a defense to intentional discrimination, the "business necessity" defense may be available in cases involving claims of illegal disparate impact discrimination. After a plaintiff presents statistical evidence showing that a neutral criterion has a significantly disproportionate negative effect on a protected class, the employer can respond that the criterion is essential to the performance of the job in question. The employer should win unless there is a less discriminatory method of ensuring that employees are able to perform the job.

Some employers, for example, have established minimum height and weight requirements for jobs, particularly in security-related jobs. These are good examples of criteria that tend to screen out significantly disproportionate numbers of women and sometimes Asians and Hispanics as well. Employers sometimes attempt to defend the criteria on the basis that the jobs require significant strength to detain prisoners, disrupt fights, and so forth. The failing in that argument, though, is that a test for strength typically is both more predictive of job success and less discriminatory than a height and weight requirement. A small but fit woman applicant may be stronger than a tall and hefty but out of shape man. Therefore, height and weight requirements often are illegal.

The types of situations that might result in disparate impact discrimination often surprise managers. A company's English-only rules, which require that all employees speak English in the workplace, may screen out individuals of a particular national origin at a disproportionate rate. A categorical bar in hiring applicants with a felony conviction may have a disparate impact because some minority groups are convicted of felonies at higher rates than the rest of the population. Requiring employees to be clean-shaven may have a disproportionate effect on African Americans who suffer from skin diseases that prevent shaving or make it very painful. All these criteria tend to result in disparate impact discrimination. That does not mean that the employer can never apply those criteria. However, the criteria must be important in predicting whether a given individual will be able to perform the job. And if there is a less discriminatory way to assess job qualifications or to achieve the same result, then that is the method the employer must use.

As a side note, the law is somewhat unclear on whether age discrimination can serve as the basis for a disparate impact claims. Some courts have decided that, although disparate impact claims can be brought based on characteristics such as race, gender, and so forth, plaintiffs alleging age discrimination must show intentional discrimination, not just disparate impact. Other courts have permitted disparate impact claims of age discrimination. The U.S. Supreme Court has not yet resolved this question. Until that happens, the conservative approach is to be sure your practices do not have a disparate impact on individuals age forty and over.

Getting At the Truth

Earlier in this section, I explained that courts have developed analytic approaches to help determine the truth in disputed cases of alleged employment discrimination. The basic approach is known as the McDonnell Douglas approach, from the name of the case where the U.S. Supreme Court first established the analysis. It has three main steps.

First, the plaintiff must establish a "prima facie" case, that is, a situation where it appears on the surface that the employer has discriminated. What the plaintiff must show in order to get to trial varies slightly, depending on the situation. However, a sample will give you a flavor of the typical requirements. In a case alleging a discriminatory termination, the plaintiff must show that (1) the plaintiff belonged to a protected class, (2) the plaintiff's job performance was acceptable, (3) other similarly situated employees in a different class were treated less harshly than the plaintiff, and (4) the plaintiff was harmed. Of these requirements, only the second and third tend to be disputed. Note that the second element, the acceptability of the employee's performance, makes it apparent why overly favorable performance evaluations can be so valuable to an employee who later experiences negative job consequences.

Assuming that a prima facie case has been established, the second step is for the employer to defend itself by stating its nondiscriminatory reason for taking the action in question. Finally, the burden shifts back to the employee to challenge the employer's explanation as a pretext for the real, illegal reason for the action.

Here a practical limit of the employment-at-will doctrine becomes apparent. Assume that a former employee is able to prove membership in a protected class (religion), a history of excellent performance evaluations, and damage in the form of dismissal from the job, while other employees of a different religion who had equivalent performance evaluations were not fired. The former employee has stated a prima facie case.

Assume next that the employer's defense is that it fired the employee not for religion but for wearing a blue shirt on a day when the employer was tired of blue. Recall from Chapter One that it is entirely legal to terminate an employee-at-will for a reason as arbitrary as this one, so long as it is not an illegal reason. The former employee can then argue that the employer's stated reason is obviously a pretext for discrimination because other employees wore blue shirts and were not fired. Now, not only is it legal for the employer to fire an employee for wearing a blue shirt, but no law requires the employer to fire everyone who wears a blue shirt simply because the employer fires one employee for that reason. The question for the jury in a discrimination case, then, is not whether the employer's stated reason is legal (it is), but whose story to believe about the employer's real motivation. Compare the employee's story—including excellent performance appraisals and different treatment of similarly situated employees of another religion—and the employer's story of the blue shirt. Whose story would you believe? In short, relying on the at-will doctrine will not necessarily save an employer where it is reasonable to believe that the real grounds of a decision constitute unlawful discrimination.

Sometimes cases are complicated by the fact that managers tend to have many reasons for making a given employment-related decision. Where the plaintiff has evidence to support an allegation that even one of the reasons underpinning a decision is illegal, then the case becomes one of "mixed motives." To avoid liability, the employer must assume the burden of proving that the manager would have made the same decision without considering the illegal motivating factor. Even then, if the plaintiff has shown that the employer's decision was influenced by race, color, religion, sex, or national origin, federal law permits the court to order prospective relief, such as an order not to consider those criteria in the future, and to award the plaintiff attorney's fees and costs.

Thus it is a fallacy that the company will avoid liability if the manager would have made the same decision without using any illegal decision-making criteria (Fact or Fallacy? item 4). In that situation, the company's liability is limited. But the bottom line is that the law still views it as inappropriate to use illegal criteria when dealing with important employment decisions.

To summarize this section on defending against charges of illegal discrimination, defenses and narrow exceptions to the law do exist. Understanding them will help you understand why some companies appear to "get away with" discrimination and why it can be so important to document and carefully evaluate legal factors when selecting a new employee, terminating a current employee, or providing other employment benefits such as training. Finally, it is useful to know that the courts have developed a specific approach to evaluate conflicting testimony in employment discrimination claims. I will not pretend that the approach gets to the truth every time. But knowing that there is a systematic pattern of analysis tends to reassure managers that all sides of the story will be heard.

■ Affirmative Action

Most managers I talk to agree in principle with the general concept of the federal nondiscrimination laws. Equal employment opportunity and the right to be evaluated on one's abilities, performance, and other relevant criteria are values that most of us seem to share. But when the subject turns to affirmative action programs, managers vary as widely in their viewpoints as does our broader society. Further, anyone who has followed the affirmative action debate in the press probably knows that the law in this area tends to be unsettled. My goal in this section is not to explain the complex nuances of the legal arguments, nor is it to take one side or the other about the use of affirmative action in employment situations, in government contracting, or in admission to educational programs. Instead, I will simply outline when employers must have affirmative action programs and the most general requirements of those programs. I will then briefly discuss some of the issues with voluntary affirmative action programs.

It is a fallacy that every employer is required to have an affirmative action program. Mandatory affirmative action programs take two forms. First, a court might order an employer that has committed egregious violations of antidiscrimination laws to engage in an affirmative action program as a remedial measure. Such orders are unusual and tend to be tailored specifically to the employer's legal violations and workforce demographics.

Second, federal regulations require every employer with at least $10,000 in government contracts and a minimum of fifty employees to meet limited affirmative action requirements, such as including specific language in job advertisements stating that the company is an equal opportunity employer. A company that has at least fifty employees and a minimum of $50,000 in government contracts must meet the same requirements and must also have a written affirmative action plan that it updates at least annually. The regulations, which were substantially simplified effective December 13, 2000, require that the affirmative action plan contain certain elements. One mandate is that the employer compare its workforce demographics to the composition of the available workforce. If the comparison shows that the employer has a disproportionately low number of minorities, women, disabled individuals, or covered veterans, then the employer must establish goals to bring the workforce more in line with the labor market.

Some employers that are not subject to the federal contractor regulations choose to have voluntary affirmative action programs. Other employers that are subject to the contractor regulations choose to be more proactive than those regulations require. In those situations, the employer's voluntary commitment to addressing what it views as important issues can be in tension with the antidiscrimination laws. It is this tension that raises the specter of "reverse discrimination." Generally, that term refers to a situation where an employer is perceived to be treating a member of a traditionally disfavored group more positively at the expense of someone who belongs to a traditionally favored group. Opponents of reverse discrimination correctly argue that the antidiscrimination laws were intended to level the playing field and outlaw discrimination based on criteria such as race, whether the victim is a member of a traditionally favored or disfavored group. On the other hand, supporters of aggressive affirmative action programs correctly argue that the antidiscrimination laws were intended to remedy problems in our society that stem from past discrimination.

Courts have to balance these strong but opposing arguments, so it is not surprising that this area of law contains many ambiguities. The courts' general approach, at this writing, is to evaluate voluntary affirmative action programs at nongovernmental employers by looking at three factors: Did the employer intend to eliminate past discrimination or underrepresentation in a traditionally segregated category of jobs? Is the plan established so that it does not unnecessarily trammel the rights of individuals who are not entitled to its benefits? Will the plan end when it achieves balance in the workforce? Only if the answer to all three questions is yes will the plan be acceptable under federal nondiscrimination laws.

To conclude this brief overview of affirmative action principles, it is a fallacy that every employer must have an affirmative action plan. Furthermore, it almost always is a fallacy to believe that the law requires hiring a person with specific characteristics for an open position or prevents the firing of a poor performer who happens to be a member of a protected group. But companies with significant government contracts, and sometimes those that have egregiously violated nondiscrimination laws, are subject to some requirements designed to ensure equal employment opportunities. In addition, while the issue of voluntary affirmative action plans remains a troubling one for the courts, some plans have been upheld as being consistent with the goals of nondiscrimination law.

■ Harassment

Nearly all managers these days know that the law forbids sexual harassment in the workplace. Unfortunately, in spite of training courses, company policies, and vast numbers of articles in the business press, most managers probably have trouble defining what might constitute sexual harassment in their workplace. This is an area that has given rise to a great many fallacies in the minds of managers and employees. It also is an area where the legal standards remain difficult to apply.

In this section, I will address some of the fallacies about harassment law. I will also discuss some of the important considerations courts appear to take into account as they decide harassment cases. Finally, I will discuss the liability rules that provide incentives for companies and managers to take actions that will minimize liability if harassment does occur.

■ Fact or Fallacy? ■

1. In the context of employment law, *harassment* refers only to sexual harassment.   ☐ Fact   ☐ Fallacy

2. Employers are legally liable for harassment of employees by managers, but not by fellow employees.   ☐ Fact   ☐ Fallacy

3. An employee who voluntarily engages in sexual relations with his or her manager may still be able to sue successfully for sexual harassment.   ☐ Fact   ☐ Fallacy

---

Evaluating Whether Harassment Exists

A common fallacy is that the law of harassment applies only to sexual harassment (Fact or Fallacy? item 1). It is illegal for people to be harassed in the workplace based on any of the traditionally protected characteristics of race, color, religion, sex, or national origin. The courts also tend to interpret newer statutes, such as the prohibition on discrimination based on disability, as making harassment on those bases illegal.

Traditionally harassment has been classified into two categories: quid pro quo claims and hostile environment claims. In quid pro quo cases, employment benefits are offered in exchange for something else, such as sexual favors. For example, in this chapter's opening scenario, the rumor mill reported that a woman named Kimdra was fired after spurning her manager's unwelcome demand for sex. Whether a manager promises employment rewards such as a promotion and pay increase in exchange for sex, or threatens an unfavorable action if the employee refuses, the employee has experienced quid pro quo sexual harassment. Other tangible employment actions that might be threatened or offered in exchange for sexual favors include such things as an initial job offer, a recall from layoff, or a demotion. Quid pro quo sexual harassment is always unlawful when the manager imposes the consequences, and a single incident is sufficient to result in a violation of federal law.

The second type of harassment claim, hostile environment, results when an employer permits unwelcome conduct to result in a work environment so discriminatory that it affects job performance or is intimidating, hostile, or offensive. It is a fallacy (Fact or Fallacy? item 2) to believe that managers are the only people who can create hostile environments. Certainly, some cases of sexual harassment do involve managers and their direct reports, but employers can also be held liable for harassment by other employees and even for harassment by customers or suppliers.

Despite what many people believe, it is irrelevant to the legal analysis whether the person who alleges harassment voluntarily engaged in conduct such as a sexual relationship with the harassing party (Fact or Fallacy? item 3). The first U.S. Supreme Court case to address a claim of sexual harassment based on hostile environment decided this exact issue. The victim's manager did not offer any specific employment benefits in exchange for sexual favors, so the issue was not one of quid pro quo. However, the victim alleged that her manager fondled her in front of co-workers and had sex with her forty or fifty times over several years. The employer argued that no illegal sexual harassment had occurred because the employee and manager had engaged in a "voluntary" relationship. In rejecting this argument, the Supreme Court stated that the applicable test in a harassment claim is not one of "voluntariness" but, instead, is whether the sexual advances are "unwelcome."[14]

This is not to say that any conduct related to a protected criterion that makes an employee uncomfortable constitutes illegal harassment. Generally, the Supreme Court has said that the alleged harassing conduct "must be sufficiently severe or pervasive 'to alter the conditions of [the victim's] employment and create an abusive working environment.'"[15] This can be a difficult determination for any manager—or court—to make. Still, there are some basic principles that are helpful to set your internal compass by if you have to evaluate a situation in your workplace.

In determining whether the conduct in question is sufficiently egregious to meet the legal standard, the courts use both a subjective and an objective test. The subjective test is whether the victim actually found the conduct problematic. So, for example, a particularly thick-skinned person who is unaffected by sexual teasing, racial slurs, or religious put-downs will not be successful in pursuing a legal claim regardless of the severity or frequency of the actions. However, even if the victim does experience the conduct as so abusive as to alter the working conditions, that alone is not enough. The courts also will apply an objective test and ask whether, depending on the court, a "reasonable person," a "reasonable person situated similarly to the victim," or a "reasonable woman" (where the victim is a woman) would have found the conduct troubling enough to change the working conditions. Consequently, an employee who is overly sensitive to teasing, slurs, or put-downs will not be successful in a harassment claim.

When I talk with managers about harassment, they tend to want something more concrete than the general principles I have just sketched, such as a "do and don't" list or a way to rank potentially harassing actions on a scale of 1 to 10. The law in this area simply does not work that way, and for good reason. The actions a person could take that might poison the working environment sufficiently to change it for someone of a particular race, color, gender, national origin, or religion are nearly infinite. So are the number of offensive jokes, slurs, or put-downs that might be in poor taste or lacking in judgment, but not so predominant in the context of the workplace that they change the working environment. Thus, it is impossible to generate a list of behaviors that fit neatly into "legal" and "illegal" categories. Instead, you have to exercise judgment in each individual situation.

I can, however, based on the concepts I have just discussed, offer some guidance as to what should go into your analysis as you weigh individual circumstances. First, be sure to look at the big picture. The legal standard refers to conduct that is "severe or pervasive." This should raise two questions in your mind. First, how egregious was the action in question? Second, how frequent or repetitive were the instances of inappropriate conduct? Finally, do not forget to evaluate the conduct from the perspective of the actual victim as well as from a more objective viewpoint.

It is possible for an action to be sufficiently egregious that one instance is enough to change the conditions of the workplace. For example, a coworker who rapes a colleague almost certainly creates an abusive working environment in the eyes of the actual victim as well as in the eyes of any reasonable person. In most cases, however, repetition is required in order to violate the law. For example, the individual who gets up the courage to ask a coworker on a date, is turned down, and does not express any further romantic interest, almost certainly does not alter the workplace conditions in the eyes of either the coworker or any reasonable person. To summarize, the Supreme Court has said that in determining whether a situation is so hostile that it violates the law, one must consider the "frequency of the discriminatory conduct; its severity; whether it is physically threatening or humiliating, or a mere offensive utterance; and whether it unreasonably interferes with an employee's work performance."[16]

Employer Liability for Harassment

Companies that want to avoid liability for sexual harassment typically take proactive measures to discourage harassment in the workplace and to minimize liability should illegal harassment occur. Also, in some instances an employee must take action within the workplace in order to win a lawsuit alleging harassment. The liability rules vary depending on two factors. The first is whether the harassers are members of management or not. The second factor is whether the victim experienced a tangible employment action.

To begin, think back to the opening scenario and the rumor Choon Lee recalled about Kimdra and Jim. The Supreme Court has made clear that if a member of management does something that causes a harassment victim to experience a tangible employment action, then the employer is liable. Put simply, in this type of case, the employer has no defense. Jim was a manager. Kimdra's termination constituted a tangible employment action. Therefore, if Jim did in fact fire Kimdra for refusing to sleep with him, the company will be liable. It becomes tremendously important, then, that companies make clear to managers that such conduct is not acceptable. Only by preventing the behavior can companies avoid liability in these situations.

A manager's actions might not result in a specific tangible employment action, but instead could constitute hostile environment harassment. This obviously assumes that the employer has been unsuccessful in preventing all workplace harassment. In such a case, the legal standards still permit the employer to avoid liability if it takes reasonable steps to prevent harassment and to quickly correct the situation if any harassment does occur, and if the victim failed to make reasonable use of the company's corrective or preventive measures. These legal standards essentially provide two strong incentives for employers and one for individuals who experience harassment.

First, the law encourages companies to take reasonable actions to actively prevent harassment in their workforces. No law requires a company to have a program to prevent harassment. However, even if an antiharassment program is not 100 percent successful in preventing hostile environment harassment by managers, simply having a program in place is one critical factor in whether the employer will win any hostile environment harassment lawsuit that results. This requires more than having a pro forma antiharassment policy in place. The policy must be specific, must provide reasonable avenues for reporting harassment, and must be communicated to employees. Together with the automatic company liability for some harassment by managers, this incentive has encouraged many companies to engage in training and communication programs about harassment-related issues. This may be one reason that, in the opening scenario, Choon's company is devoting so much attention to antiharassment and diversity.

Second, if an employee does report harassment, then the company has an incentive to respond quickly and to investigate thoroughly while respecting the rights of all the people involved—including both the victim and the alleged harasser. If the company concludes that harassment did occur, it has an obligation to take action reasonably calculated to end the harassment and that action should not penalize the victim. If you receive a complaint of harassment in your company's workforce or otherwise become aware of harassment, even if it is not in your department, this is another instance where you should swiftly seek guidance of legal counsel or the person charged with implementing your company's nondiscrimination policy. These situations often raise unique and complex issues that are beyond my ability to address in this book. But by handling the situation promptly and fairly it is likely you can bring an end to a situation that may be costly to your company in terms of both legal liability and employee morale.

From the employee's perspective, the standards encourage prompt reporting of harassment so the situation and the employer's potential liability do not escalate. Bringing harassment to the company's attention can be difficult for an employee who already might feel under siege or threatened. But the reporting requirement ensures the employer has an opportunity to address problems in its workforce and to minimize or avoid legal liability.

Finally, if the harasser is someone other than a member of management, the liability standards are a bit different. It is unlikely that anyone who is not a member of management would have the power to impose a tangible employment action. Therefore, the situation almost certainly involves hostile environment harassment. The employer will be liable if it is negligent.

As I explained in Chapter Three while discussing performance appraisals, negligence is a general legal concept that typically applies where a person or company owes a duty to act reasonably but, instead, acts in an unreasonable way that causes injury. In this context, an employer owes a legal duty to provide a workplace free of harassment. If the employer knew or should have known of the existence of harassment and failed to take adequate corrective action to end the harassment, then the employer has acted negligently. The bottom line, then, is similar to the situation where the company learns that a manager is engaging in actions that might constitute harassment. The law provides an incentive for the company to investigate and, if harassment does exist, to respond in a way that is reasonably calculated to end the harassment without penalizing the victim. In fact, one of the ways an employer is most likely to encounter trouble in defending a claim of harassment is by failing to take sufficiently timely and strict action, including firing the harasser in appropriate cases.

In summary, harassment can be difficult for managers and courts to assess. The analysis that is done by courts is fact-specific and the variety of factual situations is limited only by the imagination of would-be harassers. In this section, I have outlined some of the important considerations courts take into account, such as the severity and pervasiveness of the conduct and the effects of the harassment on the victim and on a reasonable person. In addition to this discussion of federal law, harassment victims also may bring claims under state nondiscrimination statutes and tort laws. Successful suits based on state law may significantly increase damage awards. You now should understand why so many companies take harassment complaints so seriously. By actively discouraging harassment and promptly investigating complaints, companies can often avoid legal liability while also addressing serious problems that affect morale, productivity, and turnover.

■ Balancing Issues of Religion

Workplace issues involving religious beliefs often involve unique legal analysis. This is because the law does not simply forbid discrimination based on religion, it also requires reasonable accommodation of employees' religious beliefs. One set of questions, then, involves how much accommodation a manager must make to meet the standard of reasonable accommodation. A second and potentially more troublesome question arises when one employee's religious beliefs conflict with another employee's beliefs. Whose rights must be circumscribed?

Reasonable accommodation is a fact-specific and flexible standard. Fortunately, this means that it is adaptable to the actual needs of your workplace. Unfortunately, the flexibility also means that it is somewhat unpredictable and is impossible to define or explain in a simple, concrete way. I will discuss the concept of reasonable accommodation again in the next chapter because it is also a key legal standard in determining your obligations to disabled employees. Here it is important only for you to begin to get a sense of what the legal standard requires in cases of potential discrimination based on religion.

In the context of nondiscrimination based on religion, an employer must provide a reasonable accommodation for an employee's religious beliefs so long as it does not result in an undue burden on the employer. Often the cases occur in the context of time off work for the employee to observe religious holidays. In applying the concept of undue burden, the law typically does not require employers to pay overtime or to hire an additional employee to cover the absences. If, however, the employee can switch days or shifts with another employee at a minimal cost to the employer, then that solution should be adopted.

The courts frequently are deferential to an employer that has genuinely attempted to resolve conflicts with an employee's religious beliefs. If an employee requests religious accommodations from you, then it is useful to discuss the suggested accommodations with the employee and document the discussion. The law does not require you to adopt the employee's requested approach. But, considering the approach fairly, balancing it with other possible resolutions, and documenting the process tends to be both fair and persuasive to any court that may address the issue in the future.

One question that sometimes troubles managers is what constitutes a religious belief that must be accommodated. Here, it is clear that the law protects more than just traditional precepts of well-known organized religions. The law also applies to sincerely held religious beliefs, even unusual ones, so long as they hold a place in the employee's life comparable to that fulfilled by God in traditional religions. So, for example, the EEOC has held that an employer discriminated against an employee whose religion was Wicca and who wanted to wear a pentagram and display a small cauldron in his work area. Other employees were permitted to wear and display small religious articles, but the employer illegally barred the Wiccan from engaging in similar actions.[17]

In some situations a manager must balance the requirement not to discriminate against an employee based on religion with the prohibition on religion-based harassment. This type of situation can arise, for example, when one employee feels compelled to proselytize in the workplace while other employees object to the proselytizing. Again, the cases are heavily fact dependent. If you are confronted with this type of scenario, you will want to weigh the situation, perhaps seek compromise among the employees, and possibly get advice of legal counsel. In some cases where the situation created a serious problem, the courts have upheld the decision to terminate employees who refused to limit their overt religious speech or actions.

In one case, Hewlett-Packard posted a variety of posters with employee pictures and labels such as "old," "black," or "gay." Other posters and company communications explained the company's diversity policy and encouraged tolerance and respect. Richard Peterson, a devout Christian, hung in his cubicle two Biblical passages critical of homosexuality. When Peterson refused to take them down, Hewlett-Packard fired him. Peterson sued, alleging discrimination based on religion. The court rejected his claims because Hewlett-Packard could not accommodate Peterson's beliefs in a way acceptable to him without unduly impinging upon the company's diversity policy. Although other employees were permitted to have Biblical passages in their work areas, the judge found they were not comparable to Peterson's scriptures because they did not focus on homosexuality.[18]

The prohibitions against discrimination based on religion can be summarized as generally being equivalent to the other nondiscrimination concepts I have discussed in this chapter. But as a manager, you also have a duty to reasonably accommodate religious practices so long as the accommodation does not impose an undue burden on the company. And in cases of potential religious harassment, you may need to balance difficult problems where employees hold conflicting religious beliefs.

CHAPTER SUMMARY

In this chapter I have outlined the basic principles of nondiscrimination law. Federal laws now prohibit discrimination based on race, color, religion, gender, national origin, pregnancy, age beginning at forty, disability, and military status. State laws frequently prohibit discrimination based on additional criteria. These nondiscrimination laws apply not only to decisions like hiring and firing but also to other actions that materially affect the terms, conditions, and privileges of employment.

Three major defenses are available to companies that have been accused of violating nondiscrimination laws: that discrimination has not actually occurred, that what would otherwise be illegal discrimination reflects a bona fide job qualification, and that disparate impact discrimination is a result of a business necessity. Understanding the basic workings of the defenses and the legal analysis used by courts confronted with these cases can help you evaluate difficult situations, document the rationales for employment-related decisions, and fit these laws into the broader context of employment-at-will.

Most employers are not legally obliged to have affirmative action programs. Some companies voluntarily implement affirmative action policies, but these policies must meet certain conditions to be consistent with nondiscrimination laws.

The laws governing harassment in the workplace apply not only to sexual harassment but to harassment based on any protected characteristic. Unlawful harassment includes both quid pro quo harassment by a manager and actions by anyone that create a hostile working environment. The liability standards strongly encourage employers to institute programs to discourage workplace harassment and to quickly investigate and address any harassment that does occur. Employers always remain liable, however, for harassment by managers that results in a tangible job action.

Discrimination and harassment based on religion involve some special considerations. Employers are not only obliged to avoid discrimination on religious grounds but to provide reasonable accommodation for an employee's religious beliefs. At times, it can be difficult to balance these two obligations.

Nondiscrimination laws seek to ensure equal employment opportunity in the workplace. Unfortunately, the laws can be difficult to apply. As in other areas of law discussed in this book, sound management involves much more than a narrow, legalistic perspective. Sensitivity and a genuine commitment to equal treatment of employees will help you steer clear of many thorny legal problems. More generally, many companies now devote significant resources to encouraging mutual respect in their workforces. In a climate where employees feel comfortable, companies observe increased productivity, higher morale, and reduced turnover, in addition to decreased legal liability. If you are willing and able to confront challenges to workplace tolerance, you will have added an important tool to your managerial toolkit.

Dealing with Disabilities and Lost Work Time

S arah Donrey manages a sales department at Zonar Corp.
Some of her twenty employees have serious health problems, and their time away from work has been creating
issues for the entire group. Katherine, one of the most senior
sales representatives, was diagnosed with cancer about six
months ago, and the prognosis is not good. The entire department is sympathetic with Katherine's plight. Her absences have
left the department shorthanded, though, in both leadership
and important client contacts. Meanwhile, Colin, a sales representative who joined the group about two years ago, recently
injured his back in a water-skiing accident. He was on vacation
at the time and has not returned to work. And Robert, another

of the sales representatives, has a child named Chris who is prone to illness.

Sarah is thankful that all of her employees seem to be doing the best they can given the situations they face. One of her fellow managers told her about one of his employees, who seems to be so well informed about the federal laws allowing absence and the company's policy that he takes the maximum number of days off on what the manager believes to be pretexts rather than genuine grounds for justified absence. But Sarah still worries about the operation of the department, and she wants to understand her legal obligations to employees and job candidates with illnesses and disabilities.

When I talk with managers, one of the frustrations they frequently voice concerns how to deal fairly and within the constraints imposed by law with employees forced to be absent due to health concerns—while getting their work done and keeping the rest of their staff highly motivated. Managers are well aware that they need to make accommodations for disabled employees and job candidates, but the scope of those obligations can be tough to define. Similarly, most managers have some understanding of the Family and Medical Leave Act (FMLA) and the rights it provides employees who need to be away from work due to their own or a family member's illness. When it comes to the interactions between the FMLA and federal law prohibiting discrimination based on disability, however, managers face some complex issues. Finally, workers' compensation programs and company-sponsored sick leave and disability retirement plans further muddy the picture.

In this chapter I address these issues by laying out the basic legal provisions regarding disabilities and lost work time and providing some examples. As with the other topics in this book, the legal issues in specific cases can become technically complex and turn on factual details unique to each case. My intention here is to give you an overview of the major points of the laws in this area and a sense of their application in a variety of situations so that you can continue to develop your internal compass on these issues.

■ Disabled Employees

In Chapter Four, I focused primarily on the federal antidiscrimination provisions found in Title VII, which was passed in 1967. By comparison, Congress did not enact a general law forbidding discrimination against the disabled until 1990. The relatively recent vintage of that law, the Americans with Disabilities Act (ADA), is probably one reason that managers sometimes find themselves confused about their legal obligations concerning disabled employees or job candidates. Another reason for confusion is that the ADA does not totally ban differential treatment of the disabled. Instead, in some cases it actually mandates that disabled individuals be treated differently from nondisabled individuals. Finally, it is not always clear what constitutes a disability. These aspects of the ADA can make it difficult for managers who have employees with health-related problems.

In this section, I will begin by describing the basic provisions of the ADA. Then I will consider two specialized situations. First, how should an employer treat disabled individuals who are a threat to other employees or to themselves? Second, how do the protections of the ADA apply to individuals who use illegal substances or who abuse alcohol?

■ Fact or Fallacy? ■

1. Kimberly and Karen are twin sisters who wear eyeglasses. A major airline recently denied them employment as pilots because their uncorrected vision does not meet the company's requirements. Kimberly and Karen are disabled, and the airline has illegally discriminated against them because of their disability. ☐ Fact   ☐ Fallacy

---

■ Fact or Fallacy?, Cont'd ■

2. A large manufacturing company recently modified the job requirements in its paint inspection area. It now requires employees to rotate among all four jobs in the department. If the company fires Ella, a longtime employee, because she cannot perform one of the jobs in the rotation, that firing will not violate the ADA.   □ Fact   □ Fallacy

3. William developed severe allergies to pollens indigenous to the geographic area where he worked. The allergies could not be controlled with medication. William has requested a transfer to another of the company's facilities. If the company denies William's request, it will violate the ADA.   □ Fact   □ Fallacy

4. Henry recently applied for a job that requires the use of some specific chemicals. Because of a very unusual chronic disease he has, those chemicals are likely to cause Henry severe health problems. They do not, however, represent any threat to most people. Henry still wants the job. The employer may legally refuse to hire Henry.   □ Fact   □ Fallacy

5. Amanda has a substance abuse problem that causes her to miss work and to be unable to perform her duties adequately when she does make it to work. Her employer has told her that she needs to address the problem or she will be fired. Amanda's problem is not protected by the ADA, so it would be legal to fire her.   □ Fact   □ Fallacy

---

Basic Provisions of the ADA

Most briefly and generally stated, the ADA prohibits employers from discriminating against disabled individuals who are qualified, with or without accommodation, to perform the job in question. The problem is that this seemingly simple statement hides a multitude of complexities. Also, although the ADA applies only to employers with fifteen or more employees, state laws may apply to smaller employers and sometimes contain more restrictive provisions. To fully understand your obligations to the disabled, you need to be aware of the law in your state as well as of the requirements of the ADA.

Definition of Disability Under the ADA

At its most basic the ADA protects individuals with a disability. The law is quite specific in providing that this includes individuals in any one of the following three groups: people with a physical or mental impairment that substantially limits one or more major life activities, people with a record of being substantially limited, or people who are regarded as being substantially limited. "Major life activities" include things like hearing, walking, seeing, and performing manual tasks. "Substantially limited" means that the limitation must be more than minimal. So, for example, someone with a temporary limitation, such as a broken leg that is expected to heal fully, is not entitled to protection under the ADA because a temporary limitation is not "substantial." Stated another way, the ADA does not prohibit you from discriminating against someone with a broken leg.

The situation in Fact or Fallacy? item 1, concerning twin sisters who applied for jobs as pilots at United Airlines, comes from an actual case that reached the U.S. Supreme Court. One of the major issues in the case was whether to judge the twins' health status with or without their eyeglasses. Because they were severely myopic, evaluating them while they were not wearing corrective lenses would lead to the conclusion that the twins were substantially limited in the major life activity of seeing. United Airlines argued, however, that the twins should be evaluated with their corrective lenses in place. Because the corrections provided 20/20 vision or better, accepting United Airlines' argument would mean that the twins were not disabled and therefore not protected by the ADA.

The Supreme Court agreed with United Airlines. It relied on the wording of the law as well as the limited number of

Americans—43 million—that Congress believed would be covered by the ADA at the time it passed the statute. The Supreme Court also noted that the ADA requires employers to undertake an individualized inquiry for each employee or job candidate that considers that person's abilities, health status, and so forth.

The outcome of this case surprises many managers in my executive education sessions. Because the determination of disability under the ADA applies to people in their "corrected state," and Kimberly and Karen could see well with their corrective lenses, that means that they were not disabled as defined by the statute. That, in turn, means that the ADA did not protect them. And that means that United could legally refuse to hire Kimberly and Karen because they wore glasses, even though their corrected vision was perfectly adequate for the job.[1]

Managers are also surprised by another Supreme Court case, which dealt with the situation described in Fact or Fallacy? item 2. Ella Williams sued Toyota Motor Manufacturing after she was fired because she could no longer perform her job in the paint department of an automobile assembly plant. While working at Toyota, Ella developed severe carpal tunnel syndrome impairments, and the problems appeared to be caused by her jobs in the plant. She collected workers' compensation for the injury and missed some work. For a period of time Toyota assigned her to jobs that she was able to perform. Toyota later decided that the employees in the paint department's quality control area had to rotate through all four quality control jobs. Because of her carpal tunnel problems, Ella could not perform at least one of the required jobs.

Toyota eventually fired Ella for missing work. Ella claimed that she was fired because of her disability and that Toyota failed to reasonably accommodate her in the workplace. Toyota responded that Ella was not disabled under the ADA's definition. Recall that the ADA defines a disability as a mental or physical impairment that substantially limits a major life activity.

Ella claimed that she was disabled in the major life activity of performing manual tasks. The Supreme Court, however, said that the law's use of the word "major" requires that disabilities be based on the inability to perform tasks that are central in daily life. It was not enough that Ella could not perform specific manual tasks associated with a particular job at Toyota. The Supreme Court sent the case back to the lower courts to examine this issue, but it noted that Ella "could still brush her teeth, wash her face, bathe, tend her flower garden, fix breakfast, do laundry, and pick up around the house."[2] Presumably those abilities led the Court to question whether Ella, in fact, was disabled in the sense required by the law.

If the lower courts determine that Ella is not disabled within the definition of the ADA, then the outcome will be similar to that in the twins' case against United Airlines. Ella would have no protection under the ADA, and Toyota could fire her for being unable to perform her assigned job.

Of course, in many cases it is clear that individuals are entitled to the protection of the ADA. I do not believe that any court would question whether someone with severe and uncorrectable vision or hearing impairments, someone with long-term and serious limitations on mobility, or someone with severe mental disease would qualify as disabled. As examples of the variety of health situations that can cause substantial limitations of major life functions, courts have interpreted the ADA's disability provision to protect certain individuals who are HIV positive, who have severe allergies, who have bipolar disease, who have breast cancer, and who are diabetic. In addition, EEOC regulations state that disabilities include specific learning disabilities such as dyslexia that cause an individual to be unable to read.[3] On the other hand, merely having a certain condition is not enough to qualify an individual as disabled. Where there was a lack of evidence of substantial limitation on major life functions, courts have determined that individuals with breast cancer, allergies, extreme pain when exposed to cold temperatures, color blindness, and diabetes are *not* entitled to protection under the ADA. These outcomes are consistent with the requirement that companies must make determinations of disability status on an individualized basis that evaluates the health situation of each employee and job candidate.

"Qualified Individuals" Under the ADA

Even if an individual is legally disabled under the ADA, an employer need not hire or retain someone who cannot perform essential job functions, either with or without reasonable accommodation. In the next subsection, I will discuss the law's requirement that employers provide reasonable accommodations to disabled individuals. Here, I will focus on the law's provision concerning whether the disabled individual in question is qualified for the job.

The provision that a disabled employee or job candidate be *qualified* means that employers may apply the same educational or experience standards to disabled individuals as they apply to all other individuals. Furthermore, the disabled individual must be able to perform the essential functions of the job, although reasonable accommodation may be necessary. As I discussed in an earlier chapter, courts often defer to employers and their well-drafted job descriptions when determining what functions are essential to a particular job. However, you should not be unreasonable in specifying essential functions. If the last employee to hold the job had to lift a twenty-five-pound package once during the last two years, the ability to lift that amount of weight probably is not an essential function of the job. In determining essential functions, you should consider the following factors: How frequently will the employee need to perform the task? Do other employees also perform the task? Is the task critical to achieving business objectives? Does the job exist to perform that function? Is the task associated with the expertise needed to do the rest of the job?

Consider again the case of Ella Williams and Toyota. One might think that Toyota was unreasonable in requiring Ella to be able to perform all of the jobs in paint inspection, especially since she had successfully done two of the jobs in the area for a significant period of time. The EEOC has provided specific guidance, though, on an employer's right to establish job qualifications. That guidance permits employers to change the essential functions of a position, even for people already holding the position. It also allows employers latitude in establishing an organizational structure and configuring jobs within that structure. The guidance even discusses an example where an employer requires teams of employees to be able to rotate among jobs with different functions. According to the EEOC, that type of team approach can legitimately be deemed an essential job function.[4] So Toyota's requirement that Ella be able to perform all the required functions in paint inspection appears to be appropriate under the EEOC's guidance.

"Reasonable Accommodations" Under the ADA

The concept of reasonable accommodation intersects with the ADA's requirement that disabled individuals be qualified to perform the job in question. Employers are obligated to provide a reasonable accommodation if the accommodation is necessary to enable a disabled individual to perform the essential functions of the job. It is critical, then, that you have a sense of how the law defines "reasonable accommodation" and the process to be used in evaluating accommodations. As is true in all facets of the ADA, these are highly fact-specific determinations.

The need to accommodate disabled individuals may arise in the following three contexts: the process used for job applications, the work environment or the way in which a job is performed, and equal access to benefits and privileges of employment. It is easy to provide examples of the first and third contexts. A sight-impaired person may need assistance in completing an employment application or in taking a preemployment test. Similarly, disabled employees must have access to perquisites such as an employee cafeteria and company-sponsored social events.

The more important problem facing managers typically is how to accommodate a disabled individual when the job needs to be modified in some way to enable that individual to perform the job. Here, some background is useful. If a disability is not apparent, then it is up to the individual to advise you of a disability and to request accommodation. You do not need to guess whether an employee who turns out to be unable to function in a job has physical or mental impairments that are affecting the employee's performance.

Once you observe that an employee is disabled or an employee requests accommodation, you are entitled to ask for reasonable medical documentation of the person's limitations. If you have concerns about the information provided by the employee's physician, you can require the employee to see a physician selected by the company. The law does not require you to provide the specific accommodation requested by the employee or a physician; instead it merely requires that the employee receive an effective accommodation. However, by engaging in a dialogue with the employee and by giving careful consideration to any physician's recommendations, you will be most likely to reach an effective accommodation as well as one that respects the employee's dignity and abilities. From a legal perspective, if the situation ever deteriorates into a lawsuit, I believe that an employer that can show it made honest attempts to work with the disabled employee on job accommodation is in a more favorable position than an employer that did not engage in any dialogue with the employee and instead tried to impose a unilateral solution.

An employer is not required to provide any accommodation that causes it undue hardship. Again, this is a fact-specific inquiry that depends on the financial situation, organizational structure, and business of the employer. Still, there are some general principles to keep in mind. First, if the job can be restructured or assistive equipment provided without undue hardship to the company, then you should provide that accommodation. For example, if a job requires infrequent lifting of a weight that the disabled employee is unable to lift, then perhaps an employee with an equivalent job could take over the lifting duties or special equipment could be purchased at a price affordable to the company.

By comparison, consider a job of temporary supervisor that is established to provide coverage for supervisors on any of three shifts while they are on vacation, out of work due to illness, and so forth. It seems unlikely that the essential functions of this job can be restructured in a way that would allow someone whose disability requires day shift work to perform the job. Therefore, such an applicant is not a qualified individual for the job of temporary supervisor even with accommodation, and the employer can refuse to offer the job. Similarly, in 2002, the Supreme Court decided that employers generally are not obliged to ignore their own employer-established seniority system in order to reassign a disabled employee to a job that the employee could perform.[5]

One difficulty that sometimes arises is the need for a disabled person to work a part-time or modified schedule, to work from home, or to be absent more than the norm. The EEOC guidance on this point provides that an employer is obligated to permit a disabled employee to work on a modified or part-time schedule if doing so does not represent an undue hardship to the employer. If your company has a policy of providing modified or part-time schedules in other circumstances, that is a good indication that those types of schedules do not tend to constitute an undue hardship. However, where an essential function of a job requires that a person be at work at a specific time—for example, to interact in person with other employees—then the employer can require a disabled individual to meet those requirements. More generally, however, the EEOC takes the position that attendance is not an essential function of jobs and that an employer must accommodate a disabled person's need to be absent from work due to the disability. Many courts that have addressed the issue disagree and have recognized that it may be an undue burden for an employer to retain an employee who cannot regularly perform the functions of the assigned job.

The bottom line, as in any situation where the law is unclear, depends on the amount of risk you and your company are willing to assume. The worst-case scenario is that a court will not permit you to terminate a disabled person who is absent because of disability. The only way you can be absolutely sure of avoiding legal liability, then, is by not terminating the employee. However, if the absenteeism is severe, is imposing unacceptable costs on your company, and courts in your area have permitted other employers to fire disabled employees for absenteeism, then you may decide to accept the risk of a lawsuit. In these cases, where legal standards vary throughout the country or are still being developed, it can be especially useful to obtain legal advice before making a final decision.

Basics of the ADA: A Summary Example

To summarize the key concepts of the ADA, consider the situation of William Woods, who worked as a truck driver at United Parcel Service (UPS) in Austin, Texas. This case is the basis of Fact or Fallacy? item 3, although the actual facts are slightly more complex. After Woods developed severe allergies to a type of tree called Mountain Cedar, he requested that UPS transfer him to northern Kentucky, where Mountain Cedar does not grow. UPS refused because it had a company policy against transfers. Allegedly, though, supervisors at UPS suggested to Woods that he resign, move, and reapply to a UPS facility in his new area. But when Woods followed that advice, UPS refused to hire him due to its company policy against rehiring former employees. Woods complained to the EEOC, which brought suit against UPS on his behalf, alleging in part that UPS had not made a reasonable accommodation of Woods's disability.

This case raises all of the analytical principles I have just outlined. First, was Woods disabled and therefore entitled to the protection of the ADA? As you now know, it is incorrect to categorize people with allergies as either all entitled to protection under the ADA or as all unprotected. Some people may have allergies that do not substantially impair their ability to engage in major life activities such as breathing or walking. Other people may have more severe allergies, but if those allergies can be controlled by medication, then the principles of the case of the twin sisters tell us that those people are to be evaluated considering the effect of the medication. If, with medication, they are not substantially impaired in their ability to engage in major life activities, then they are not entitled to protection under the ADA. Other individuals, however, may have severe allergies that do substantially impair major life activity and that cannot be controlled with medication. This was Woods's situation. Evidence indicated that, by the time he requested the transfer, he rarely left home and spent most of his time there in bed because of the severity of his condition.

If you determine that an individual is disabled within the meaning of the ADA and thus entitled to the law's protections, the next question you should consider is whether the individual is qualified for the job. In Woods's case, there was no real question of his basic qualifications as a driver. He worked as a UPS driver from January 1984 through October 1994. During that time, "his record at UPS was unblemished and he later received positive letters of recommendation from his supervisor in Texas."[6]

Since Woods was both disabled and qualified for the job, the remaining question the court faced was the extent of the company's obligation to accommodate Woods by transferring him to another UPS facility. Assuming that Woods's story was true, he did make UPS aware of his disability, and he requested accommodation. Although UPS denied his request for transfer, it offered an alternative accommodation—an opportunity to resign and be rehired at a new location where the source of his allergies would not exist. The court noted that the interaction Woods and UPS apparently engaged in to try to reasonably accommodate his disability was exactly the type of process encouraged by the regulations.

UPS, however, argued that after Woods resigned his job in Texas, he no longer was entitled to any protection under the ADA. Moreover, since Woods resigned voluntarily, UPS had not imposed any negative employment action on him. The court rejected this argument. It found that, if Woods had resigned only as a step suggested by UPS in accommodating his disability, then his resignation was not truly voluntary. The court also noted, consistent with other courts and the EEOC guidance, that an employer must "consider transferring a disabled employee who can no longer perform his old job even with accommodation to a new position within the Company for which that employee is otherwise qualified."[7] In short, Woods had a prima facie case, and the court remanded the case for trial, where the facts of the case would be argued. The court's action suggests that our Fact or Fallacy? item 3 is true—an employer who refused to transfer an employee in these circumstances could be in violation of the ADA.

The ADA and Direct Threat of Harm

In rare circumstances, you also must consider the implications of the ADA when dealing with employees or job candidates who pose risks to others or to themselves. I will first discuss situations where the risk is to people other than the disabled employee or candidate. Second, I will explain the ADA provisions that apply when employees or applicants pose a risk to themselves.

Threats to Others

All of us are aware of violent episodes in the workplace that have resulted in the death of employees. Some of the perpetrators of violence have been employees, former employees, or job candidates who suffered from mental health problems. As a general matter, the ADA protects individuals with mental impairments that substantially limit a major life function. This means that you cannot discriminate in the workplace against people with severe diagnosed mental conditions who are able to perform the essential functions of their jobs with or without accommodation. But does this also mean that you cannot take action if a disabled individual represents a current and real threat to others in the workplace?

The answer is a resounding no. The language of the ADA is specific: in applying qualification requirements for a job, employers "may include a requirement that an individual shall not pose a direct threat to the health or safety of other individuals in the workplace."[8] This language makes it clear that an employer may refuse to hire individuals whose mental condition would make them a direct threat to others.

Similarly, the courts have supported employers in firing a disabled employee who has threatened fellow workers. In one case, an employee who suffered from major depression and paranoid disorder telephoned her office and said, among other things, that she was "ready to kill" her boss. As a result the employer fired her. She then sued, claiming that her mental disability caused her threatening behavior and that the employer should have accommodated her disability by providing guards to keep her from "getting out of hand." The court determined that the proposed accommodation would be an undue burden on the employer and would create undue anxiety among her coworkers.[9]

In addition to risks associated with violent behavior, an individual's physical or medical condition may create a risk to others if the condition prevents the individual from safely performing the job. For example, if the driver of the company's shuttle van has epilepsy that cannot be controlled with medication, the potential of having a seizure while driving will increase the risk of traffic accidents. Under the legal provisions I have already discussed, the employer would seem to have a clear right to fire the driver, or to refuse to hire someone with this condition for the job in question.

Rarely, though, are legal standards simple, even when the language of a statute seems clear. And, as with all ADA situations, in the case of a disabled person who might pose a direct threat to others, you still need to evaluate the specific situation on an individualized basis. EEOC guidance advises that you consider the following:[10]

- Does the individual pose a significant risk of substantial harm?
- Can you identify a specific risk associated with the disability?
- Is the risk current rather than speculative or remote?
- Is your evaluation based on objective factual evidence, such as a physician's statement?

These considerations ensure that you go through a careful process of evaluating each individual case. As an example, the EEOC cites the disability of someone with epilepsy who during the last year has lost consciousness due to seizures. Although the person might pose a significant and current risk of substantial harm to others if hired as a shuttle bus driver, the person may be able to hold a clerical position. In contrast, another applicant may have epilepsy that is well controlled by medication and have no recent record of seizures. That person may be qualified for the job of shuttle bus driver.

Threats to the Disabled Employees Themselves
Cases where employees' or applicants' disabilities pose a workplace threat only to themselves and not to fellow employees troubled the courts for a time. Consider the wording of the relevant provision of the ADA: employers "may include a requirement that an individual shall not pose a direct threat to the health or safety of other individuals in the workplace."[11] That language does not clearly resolve the situation where the only risk is to the disabled employee.

In 2002, the Supreme Court addressed this question in the case that served as the basis for Fact or Fallacy? item 4, involving Mario Echazabal. Echazabal worked at a Chevron U.S.A. refinery, but he was employed by an outside contractor. He applied twice for a job with Chevron but could not pass Chevron's physical examination. Echazabal had liver damage attributable to hepatitis C, and Chevron's physicians determined that being exposed to chemicals in the refinery could cause his condition to deteriorate. As a result, Chevron refused to hire him. Echazabal sued, alleging that Chevron had illegally discriminated against him due to his disability.

The Supreme Court decided that it was unclear from the statutory language whether Congress meant for disabled individuals to be able to assume risks to themselves that might result from specific jobs. However, EEOC guidance did permit employers to consider the risk employees or applicants might pose to themselves. This is consistent with employers' reasonable interests in avoiding the liability, loss of work time, increased health care costs, and so forth that would be associated with situations where a workplace factor severely aggravates an existing disability. Furthermore, protecting all individuals from negative health consequences in the workplace conforms with goals of federal health and safety laws. The Court did make clear, however, that even in this type of case employers have an obligation to engage in an "'individualized assessment of the individual's present ability to safely perform the essential functions of the job,' reached after considering, among other things, the imminence of the risk and the severity of the harm portended."[12] Thus it is likely in Fact or Fallacy? item 4 that the employer legally may refuse to hire Henry after conducting an individualized assessment of the risk and potential harm.

The ADA and Alcohol Abuse and Illegal Drug Use

Managers frequently question me about how the ADA applies to employees or applicants who have substance abuse problems. This is an area that the law addresses with some specificity. The ADA explicitly says that it does not protect individuals who are "currently engaging in the illegal use of drugs."[13] So an employee can be fired, and an applicant can be denied a job, on the basis of current illegal use of drugs. The ADA also permits employers to prohibit employees from using, or being under the influence of, alcohol and illegal drugs while in the workplace.[14]

Another question I am sometimes asked is whether managers must depart from the company's standards when evaluating the conduct or performance of employees who have alcohol abuse problems or who engage in illegal drug use. Again, the answer is no. The ADA permits employers to hold employees with these types of substance abuse problems to the same performance standards and expectations regarding proper conduct in the workplace as the employer applies to other employees.[15] Thus in the last of the Fact or Fallacy? items, Amanda's manager can indeed require that she meet the same performance standards required of other employees and fire her if she does not.

However, the ADA does contain some provisions designed to encourage individuals with substance abuse problems to seek help and to protect against erroneous employer stereotyping. Employers may not discriminate against an individual who has successfully completed a supervised rehabilitation program, or who is currently participating in such a program and who is not currently engaging in the illegal use of drugs. Similarly, the ADA prohibits an employer from discriminating against a person the employer erroneously regards as engaging in illegal use of drugs.

Numerous employers now provide employee assistance programs to aid employees who face problems with alcohol abuse or illegal drug use. Not only do these programs assist employees with difficult problems, they may help to minimize lost productivity and the loss of skilled employees. As a manager, you should be aware of the programs your company offers as well as of the law in this area.

■ Lost Work Time

A frequent concern I hear from managers involves the challenges they face in dealing with lost work time due to employee illness or health problems in the employee's family. The most significant federal law affecting managers' actions in this area is the Family and Medical Leave Act (FMLA). In this section, I discuss the most common issues managers have in applying this law.

■ Fact or Fallacy? ■

1. An employee who misses two days of work to care for a very ill child is entitled to FMLA leave. □ Fact □ Fallacy

2. An employee who misses four consecutive days of work due to a serious illness is entitled to FMLA leave; it is not necessary for the employee to see a physician. □ Fact □ Fallacy

3. If a company provides paid sick leave, an employee can use all of that paid leave entitlement before going on FMLA leave. □ Fact □ Fallacy

---

■ **Fact or Fallacy?, Cont'd** ■

4. An employee who is injured at work cannot
   sue the employer for negligence and still collect
   workers' compensation.   □ Fact   □ Fallacy

5. An employee who is injured after attending a
   company-sponsored social event is entitled to
   collect workers' compensation.   □ Fact   □ Fallacy

In many situations managers attempt to be as flexible as possible with employees who have serious health problems or who have close family members with severe problems. But it is also important to understand the requirements imposed by federal law as well as any additional obligations under state or local law. At employers with at least fifty employees, the FMLA guarantees employees the right to take unpaid time off work of up to twelve weeks in a twelve-month period for "serious health conditions" experienced by the employee or an immediate family member, or for the birth, adoption, or foster care placement of a child.

Typically, when an employee returns to work after FMLA leave, the employer must return the employee to the same job held prior to the leave, or to an equivalent job. There is an exception in the law, however, that permits employers to replace "key" employees—defined as being among the most highly compensated 10 percent of employees—whose leaves would cause grievous and substantial economic injury to the employer. The company is permitted to verify the severity of the health condition to ensure the employee is entitled to FMLA leave. In addition, if the leave is based on planned medical treatment such as foreseeable surgical procedures, the employee must provide the employer with thirty days' advance notice of the leave.

The two FMLA-related difficulties I most often hear about from managers involve defining what medical problems meet the law's definition of a "serious health condition" and the need of some employees to take intermittent leaves. In combination, the law and regulations provide that medical conditions qualify under the act as "serious health conditions" when they require inpatient medical care or absence from school or work for more than three days and at least two or more visits to a health care provider. Consider the first two Fact or Fallacy? items in light of this legal standard. An employee who is off work for two days to care for an ill child and takes the child to a physician on each of those days does not qualify for leave. Likewise, an employee who misses work for four days, but who does not see a physician, does not qualify for FMLA leave. Thus, both Fact or Fallacy? statements are fallacies.

FMLA also guarantees employees the right to take sporadic leaves required for treatment such as chemotherapy or to work part-time schedules required while phasing back into work after a serious illness. If you have an employee who needs to take intermittent leave or to work a part-time schedule, you may transfer the person to a position with equivalent pay and benefits that is adaptable to the person's work schedule.

The law is quite specific in its provisions concerning pay and benefits for employees on FMLA leave. First, you are not required to pay employees who are on FMLA leave. If the employee is working a part-time schedule and is on FMLA for the remaining hours of a full-time schedule, then the law only requires you to pay the employee for the time actually worked. You must, however, maintain health care coverage for an employee who is on FMLA leave. If the company benefit plan requires employees to contribute to the cost of health care coverage, the company may also apply that requirement to employees on FMLA leave.

If your company provides paid sick leave as part of its employee benefit programs, then either the employee or the company can decide that the paid sick leave and FMLA run concurrently. Typically it is the employer that designates the two leaves to run concurrently. This is the general question raised by the third Fact or Fallacy? item. So, for example, if your company's policy allows six weeks of paid sick leave and an employee expects to be out of work for eight weeks, the employee cannot unilaterally use all the sick leave first and then go on FMLA leave. Instead, the company can elect to treat the first six weeks as both paid sick leave and FMLA. The last two weeks would be unpaid FMLA leave. Ignoring any other leaves or factors, the employee would then be entitled to four more weeks of FMLA leave during the year.

The ability to designate FMLA leave to run concurrently with sick leave can be an advantage to a manager who cannot afford to maintain an open position for an employee with a long-term health problem. Consider the case of an employee who needs to be off work for sixteen weeks at a company that provides for six weeks of paid leave. If the six weeks of paid leave runs consecutively with twelve weeks of FMLA leave, the employee would be entitled to be off work for a total of eighteen weeks. By designating the leaves as running concurrently, the company has the legal right to terminate an employee who remains totally disabled and cannot return to work after twelve weeks.

The provisions of FMLA that I have described are minimum provisions and do not prevent you from providing employees with more generous leaves. If, however, you consider voluntarily providing different employees with leaves of varying lengths or conditions, you should evaluate whether your actions might violate the nondiscrimination provisions I have discussed earlier. Are you treating people differently because of health conditions that qualify as disabilities? If so, you will want to consider the provisions of the ADA, which may provide a legal basis for the differential treatment. Or is the real reason you are treating people differently because of characteristics such as gender, race, or religion? If so, your actions may violate Title VII or other nondiscrimination laws. And, as always, you must consider the effect of any applicable state and local laws.

■ Employees with Work-Related Injuries

The workers' compensation system in the United States developed as a compromise for both employers and employees. For employees, the system provides protection in case of injuries associated with work. When an employee is injured because of and in the course of employment, that employee is entitled to receive workers' compensation. Those payments may be made as a lump sum amount for the permanent loss of bodily function, such as the loss of a finger, or they may be in the form of replacement of some amount of the salary that would otherwise be lost while the employee is off work due to the injury. Although workers' compensation programs are mandatory, and employers must choose either to pay premiums to state programs or private insurers or to self-insure, employers gain a significant benefit as well: they are protected against most lawsuits an employee otherwise might be entitled to bring under theories such as negligence. So, in answer to the Fact or Fallacy? item 4, an employee who is entitled to receive workers' compensation typically is precluded from suing the employer on other legal theories.

Workers' compensation laws exist primarily at the state level, and there is significant variation among the states. In general, though, state laws do tend to specify the amount of lump sum payment an individual is entitled to because of permanent impairment. State laws also specify the amount of weekly wage replacement an individual is entitled to, and those amounts tend to be capped at relatively modest levels.

Most situations involving injury to an employee at work are relatively clear and raise few legal questions. In unusual cases, however, managers may dispute an individual's entitlement to workers' compensation. The legal standards governing the employee's entitlement to workers' compensation typically require that the worker be injured; the injury arose out of employment, meaning that the employment caused the injury; and the injury occurred during the course of employment. The last requirement is analyzed based on the time, place, and circumstances of the accident. Some disputed cases occur when an employee is injured at or after a company-sponsored event that is, at least in part, a social event.

As an example, Pepsi-Cola Bottling Company employed David Allison as a driver-salesperson. The company sponsored a ten-week sales promotion program that rewarded drivers with "fun" money. The only way a driver could use the money was by attending a Vegas Night party set up by the company. David consumed numerous drinks before and during the party. On his way home, David died in a car accident. His widow claimed workers' compensation benefits. Pepsi-Cola argued that David was not acting as an employee when he attended the party, and that, even if the court disagreed on the first point, David voluntarily consumed so much alcohol that his actions were unrelated to his employment.

The Michigan Court of Appeals first determined that David was indeed acting as an employee. The court found that the employer derived a clear benefit from sponsoring Vegas Night and that employees were expected to attend the party. After all, only by attending could employees use the awards they received during the sales promotion. Further, testimony indicated that the branch manager told drivers that "you better be there."[16]

Nor did the court believe that David had departed from his employment while driving home. Typically, commuting to and from work is not considered part of employment. So, in the normal course of events, an employee injured during the daily drive to the office is not eligible for workers' compensation. The court viewed David's situation as being different, however. David was not driving to or from his normal place of work when the accident occurred. Instead, he "was attending a special function at this employer's request and benefit and was in the course of his employment while there."[17]

Pepsi-Cola's second argument was that, by drinking so heavily, David had deviated so significantly from what was required by his job that he was no longer acting "in the course of his employment." The court rejected this argument on the basis that most of David's drinking occurred at the employer party. The court therefore awarded workers' compensation benefits to David's widow.

To sum up, if one of your employees is injured while at work, that employee is most likely entitled to workers' compensation benefits under state law. That coverage, however, extends only to employees and not to independent contractors or other nonemployee workers. In cases where the relationship between the employee's injury and work is attenuated, the analysis is likely to depend on two factors. First, did the injury arise out of the individual's employment? That is, was employment the cause of the accident? Second, did the injury occur within the scope of employment? That is, was it within the time, space, and circumstances of employment? If the answer to both of these questions is yes, then the employee most likely is entitled to workers' compensation.

■ Conclusion

The situations Sarah faces in the scenario that opened this chapter illustrate some of the complexities raised by the ADA, the FMLA, and the interaction of these laws with company-sponsored sick leave policies. Recall that Katherine, a senior sales representative, was diagnosed with cancer and that her absences have left the department shorthanded. For Sarah, Katherine's situation raises questions under the FMLA, the ADA, and the company's sick leave policy. Since her prognosis is not good, and assuming she is undergoing continuing medical treatment, Katherine's condition seems to qualify as a serious health condition under FMLA standards. As a result, she is entitled to twelve weeks of unpaid leave per year. She may take the leave intermittently if her health and treatment require those absences. To the extent that Zonar Corp. has a paid sick leave program, either Katherine or Zonar may designate the sick leave to run concurrently with FMLA leave. Zonar must maintain Katherine's company-paid health care coverage while she is on FMLA leave. If Katharine's cancer forces her to miss more than twelve weeks of work, and company policy does not provide otherwise, then Zonar may terminate her employment without violating the FMLA.

As Katherine's manager, though, Sarah must also consider the requirements of the ADA. You now know that each employee's health status must be examined individually in order to determine if the employee is disabled within the meaning of the ADA. A cancer diagnosis does not automatically qualify an individual as being disabled under that law, and the facts in the opening scenario are too sketchy to permit a final decision on this point. However, the facts do tell us that Katherine's diagnosis occurred six months ago and that the prognosis is not good. Moreover, it appears she is so ill that she is missing substantial amounts of work. Those factors indicate there is some likelihood that Katherine's cancer is substantially limiting a major life activity and that she is not likely to return to good health in the near term. If that is true, then she is disabled and entitled to the protections of the ADA.

We have already established that Zonar may be able to terminate Katherine's employment consistent with the FMLA. If Katherine is disabled, however, then the ADA requires Sarah to determine whether Katherine can perform the essential functions of her job with or without accommodation. If Katherine can satisfactorily perform her job while working from home part of the time or during nonstandard business hours, then it may be a reasonable accommodation for Sarah to permit her to do so. If Katherine's current position is not compatible with her disability, then perhaps there is an open position at Zonar where Katherine could perform satisfactorily. In short, the ADA requires Zonar to provide Katherine with reasonable accommodation to permit her to perform the essential functions of a job at Zonar if such a job is available. Because of the long-term nature of this particular situation, the ADA appears to be more protective than the FMLA of Katherine's employment rights.

Colin's back injury raises many of the same issues for Sarah and Zonar as Katherine's cancer. Back injuries, however, fall into a category of health issues, along with severe headaches, certain mental disabilities, and chronic fatigue syndrome, that can be very difficult to treat. These health issues are further complicated by difficulties in assessing the severity of the disease or injury and the level of continuing impairment attributable to the disease or injury. If Sarah suspects that Colin may actually be able to return to work, she may require him to provide medical evidence of his condition from his own physician and may require him to see another physician for verification purposes.

Robert's situation raises issues only under the FMLA. The ADA does not provide any protection to a nondisabled employee with an ill or disabled child. However, if Robert's child's illness meets the FMLA's definition of "serious health condition," then Robert is entitled to up to twelve weeks' leave in a twelve-month period to care for the child.

In some ways, situations involving ill or injured employees, or employees whose family members experience medical problems, can be among the most difficult issues you face as a manager. Not only is an employee with these problems entitled to the protections of various laws, but it is natural for all of us to want to provide whatever aid and assistance we can. On the other hand, as a manager you face practical problems in ensuring that necessary work functions are completed, that unscrupulous employees do not misuse the system, and that you are able to treat employees facing unique and difficult situations fairly, humanely, and in a nondiscriminatory fashion. Understanding the basic legal principles that apply in these circumstances will not make these situations easy to deal with, but it will help you make more informed decisions.

CHAPTER SUMMARY

The ADA applies to job applicants and employees who have a mental or physical condition that meets its definition of disability. Managers cannot discriminate against disabled individuals who can perform the necessary function of the job, with or without accommodation. Determining whether a person is disabled but able to perform necessary job functions, and the nature of any accommodation needed to permit performance, requires individualized analysis. The lack of precise standards frustrates some managers. But it does provide flexibility and encourages managers to work with employees and job candidates to reach a result that is good for both the company and the worker.

One area where the law is clear is in situations where an employee, even a disabled employee, poses a risk of harm to other employees, customers, or suppliers. In such a situation, the manager should eliminate the threat or terminate the employee who poses the threat. Furthermore, a manager may refuse to hire or may fire a person when continued employment poses an imminent risk of severe harm to that person.

The ADA provides only limited protections in the area of alcohol and illegal drug use. Basically, the provisions prevent negative stereotyping and help provide incentives for people with these types of problems to seek treatment. However, a manager may hold employees with illegal drug use and alcohol abuse issues to the same performance expectations as imposed on other employees. Those individuals also may be terminated or disciplined for using or being under the influence of alcohol or illegal drugs while at work.

The FMLA permits employees to take up to twelve weeks unpaid leave during a twelve-month period for a "serious health condition" of their own or of a member of their immediate family. It also applies in certain situations when a child joins the family. The company can designate that FMLA leave runs concurrently with a company-sponsored sick leave program.

Employees with work-related injuries typically are entitled to workers' compensation payments. Workers' compensation programs exist at the state level and vary somewhat from state to state. As a general matter, though, employees get workers' compensation benefits for injuries that arise out of employment and during the scope of employment.

Managers frequently confront situations with disabled, ill, or injured employees that challenge their ability to maintain productivity, get necessary work completed, and meet deadlines. Illness, disability, or injury of a member of an employee's family may raise similar issues. In some of these circumstances, personal crises spill over into the workplace. If you face this type of situation, you probably will be forced to balance the employee's individual needs with business pressures. Among the factors to consider in your decision-making process are the applicable laws discussed in this chapter.

Terminating Employees

R ichard manages a department at Abcure Corporation that includes employees who work in the field as well as at headquarters. In an effort to deal with rising costs of its health care insurance program, Abcure recently announced an increase in co-pays and in the contributions some employees must make to the basic premium costs. In an effort to mitigate the bad news, Abcure also announced some improvements in the health insurance program.

One of Richard's employees, Donna, responded to the changes by sending her fellow employees in the division a vitriolic e-mail message deriding the modifications and comparing Abcure's health care coverage unfavorably to that offered by its competitors. In her e-mail, Donna encouraged people to complain to their managers in an effort to convince Abcure to rescind the changes. Donna's message angered the vice president in charge of benefits, who insisted that Donna be fired for insubordination.

Another employee, Kolbe, recently complained to Richard that Jergen keeps calling him into Jergen's workspace to look at porn Web sites. Kolbe is not comfortable with what Jergen is doing, especially since Kolbe knows that Abcure has a policy about appropriate use of e-mail and the Web. Richard is trying to decide what to do about Kolbe's complaint.

Last, Stewart, a field representative, was in an accident and totaled his new company car while traveling from one client meeting to another. Neither Stewart nor anyone else was hurt, but it appears that Stewart was speeding at the time and was at fault for the accident. This did not particularly surprise Richard, who knows that Stewart is an aggressive individual. It is that very aggressiveness that makes Stewart one of Richard's top performers. A human resources person has asked to meet with Richard and Stewart about the accident. Apparently he is concerned that the company may be liable if Stewart has another accident and injures someone.

In this final chapter, I focus on legal issues in terminating employees. In some ways this chapter is a review and summary of everything you have already learned. After all, any analysis of a manager's right to terminate an employee begins with the principle of employment-at-will and its limitations. For that reason, I begin this chapter with a final discussion of employment-at-will.

I also ask you here, though, to apply your knowledge to new contexts. More and more employers in recent years have confronted employees' misuse of e-mail and Internet technology. I will discuss the issues of employee privacy and potential employer liability raised by situations like those involving

Donna and Kolbe in the opening scenario. Next, I will briefly discuss the federal laws protecting the right of employees to act collectively. Because of the low rates of unionization in this country, I do not cover labor law in any depth in this book. However, every manager needs to be aware of a few basic concepts, including the fact that the so-called labor union laws protect most nonmanagerial employees whether or not they are unionized or are trying to unionize.

I will then turn to questions, illustrated by the example of Stewart, concerning the potential liability your company faces if one of your employees injures someone who is not an employee. I will close the chapter with a brief discussion of some of the procedural and practical considerations managers face when terminating employees.

■ Employment-at-Will and Its Exceptions: A Review

As you know, employment-at-will is a basic concept in U.S. employment law. In prior chapters, I focused on applying this concept to hiring, promotions, and performance evaluations. Here I will review the principles from earlier in the book and apply them specifically in situations involving employee termination.

The basic idea is simple enough: as a manager, you have the right to terminate an employee at any time, for any reason, even a lousy, unfair, or arbitrary reason, or for no reason at all, so long as it is not an illegal reason. This principle allows managers great discretion in dealing with their employees. However, the exceptions are extensive, and they can be difficult to apply in specific circumstances.

In Chapter One, I discussed three exceptions to employment-at-will: contracts, nondiscrimination laws, and policy-based and statutory provisions. All three exceptions are important in evaluating whether you may legally terminate an employee.

■ Fact or Fallacy? ■

---

1. The owners of PCC meet with Mueller to discuss Mueller's possible employment at PCC. The owners explain their expansion goals over the next two to four years. Mueller makes it clear that he believes it will take three or four years to build client relationships. If PCC then hires Mueller, Mueller can rely on this discussion as an implied contract of employment for at least three years.   □ Fact   □ Fallacy

2. Arlando was injured while working and provided his employer with a doctor's statement that he would be off work indefinitely due to the injury. The employer fired Arlando after he did not comply with a company policy that required employees to call in prior to 9 A.M. on any day they would miss work. Given the doctrine of employment-at-will, the company is legally within its rights to fire Arlando.   □ Fact   □ Fallacy

3. Mega Corporation is planning to significantly downsize its workforce because of increasing competition and decreasing demand for its products. As long as the company is careful to steer clear of illegal criteria, such as discriminatory ones, it may use any basis it wishes, no matter how arbitrary, in selecting the employees to let go.   □ Fact   □ Fallacy

---

Employment-at-Will and the Contract Exception

To begin, consider the situation outlined in the first Fact or Fallacy? item. When Dennis and Kathy Gamble, the owners of PCC, met with Joseph Mueller about the possibility of employing Mueller, they discussed their plans for PCC's expansion over the next two to four years. According to a published report, "Mueller told the Gambles that it would take three to four years to build relationships with clients that would be beneficial to PCC in the future."[1] The Gambles and Mueller first negotiated a temporary contract of employment and then a final one. The final contract contained a five-year noncompete clause and some provisions, including one regarding potential ownership rights, negotiated by Mueller. Neither contract contained any provisions regarding the duration of employment.

PCC terminated Mueller's employment after nine months. Mueller sued PCC, alleging, among other things, breach of contract. He argued that the discussion of the Gambles' two-to-four year plans for expansion and his statement that it would take three to four years to build appropriate client relationships implied the existence of a three-year contract of employment. The court, however, disagreed and decided that Mueller was an employee-at-will. The court recognized that the parties' discussions would have had to be much more specific and clear in order to constitute a contract for a specific duration of employment. Since Mueller was an employee-at-will and did not allege he had been fired for an illegal reason, the court upheld his termination.[2]

As I discussed in Chapter One, verbal promises to employees may be enforceable. It is important not to make promises to your employees that you cannot or do not intend to keep. On the other hand, this case shows that the law recognizes the importance of general long-term planning discussions and that promises must be fairly specific to constitute enforceable contracts. Nevertheless, as a manager you should keep the principles of implied verbal contracts in mind as you engage in discussions of future business goals or other job-related matters with employees and job candidates.

Employment-at-Will and the Public Policy Exception

The second Fact or Fallacy? scenario illustrates a public policy exception to employment-at-will. Arlando Redricks was injured in the course of his job at Industrial Vehicles International. I am simplifying the facts of the actual case a bit, but basically his supervisor committed the company's existing policy, which required absent employees to phone in daily prior to 9 A.M., to writing. That written notice specified that if an employee did not phone in for five consecutive days, the employee would be terminated. The supervisor distributed the written notice to employees while Arlando was out of work due to the injury and did not send him a copy. Arlando called in daily early during his absence. He then provided Industrial Vehicles with a physician's certificate of disability indicating that Arlando would be off work indefinitely. At that point Arlando stopped making the daily calls. Industrial Vehicles fired Arlando for not complying with its company policy.

Arlando sued, arguing that the state's workers' compensation statute protected him from being fired while he was absent due to a work-related injury. The statute in Oklahoma provided that "No person, firm, partnership, corporation, or other entity may discharge any employee during a period of temporary total disability solely on the basis of absence from work."[3] The company responded that it did not fire Arlando because of his absence or because of his workers' compensation claim, but instead because of his failure to call in as required by company policy. Industrial Vehicles believed that the principles of employment-at-will permitted it to fire him for that reason. The appellate court, however, held for Arlando. In its own words: "Given the public policy involved, we find that a requirement reduced to writing but never sent to an absent employee, who was exercising a statutory right, is unduly burdensome given the employer's justification for the requirement."[4] To me the supervisor's actions appear to retaliate against Arlando for collecting workers' compensation. As I discussed earlier, retaliation against employees who are exercising legal rights is one type of managerial action the law does not tolerate.

Contrast another case where an employee argued that her termination violated a public policy exception to employment-at-will. Linda Rowan, an administrative cashier at Tractor Supply Company, confronted her manager, Jerry Snider, with her belief that he and others were embezzling from TSC. Snider responded "violently by twisting [Linda's] arm and pushing her forcefully against the desk."[5] When Linda complained to TSC management, she was repeatedly told to keep quiet and not pursue the matter. Linda, however, filed both civil and criminal complaints against Snider for the physical attack. After she won her civil suit, TSC advised Linda that she should drop the criminal charges. When she refused, TSC fired her before the criminal trial, during which Snider was convicted of assault and battery.

Linda sued TSC, alleging that her termination violated Virginia's public policy against obstruction of justice because it was intended to discourage her from testifying and to get her to drop the criminal charges. TSC, on the other hand, argued that Linda was an at-will employee and no public policy or statutory exception to employment-at-will prevented TSC for firing Linda for any reason, even for refusing to drop criminal charges against a manager who physically attacked her at work. The court agreed with TSC and upheld Linda's termination.

In its decision, the court reminds us that only narrow exceptions exist to the principle of employment-at-will. Furthermore, the court distinguished this situation from cases where statutes such as nondiscrimination laws specifically grant rights to individuals or embody clear principles, such as protecting the general public from crime (so that, for example, employees who refuse to commit crimes at their employer's direction are protected against termination). The policy inherent in the obstruction of justice statute protects the public from a "flawed legal system."[6] It has no bearing on an individual's "right" to be free from being terminated from a job.

Taken together, the cases brought by Linda and Arlando illustrate the fact that public policy exceptions to the doctrine of employment-at-will do exist, but that they tend to be narrow. Nor will your common sense or your intuitions about fairness necessarily agree with what the law dictates. As you evaluate specific situations in your workplace, you should consider whether terminating an employee for the reason you are considering might be inconsistent with the policies and goals of the laws and legal mores in your jurisdiction. At times this will require more knowledge than most managers have of the law. If you are unsure whether your situation conflicts with principles embodied in the legal system, then you may want professional advice from an employment law attorney about the level of risk associated with a potential termination.

Employment-at-Will and Mass Terminations

The concept of employment-at-will remains generally applicable in situations where large numbers of employees are terminated, such as the downsizing that is the topic of Fact or Fallacy? item 3. That means an employer may select employees to be let go according to any criteria that do not violate the law—or even randomly.

Practically, though, because large-scale terminations can generate significant animosity among those let go as well as morale problems among those who remain, most employers apply rational criteria when reducing their workforces, such as length of service or performance evaluations. Besides, employers faced with the necessity of downsizing tend to want to retain their most productive employees and therefore have even more incentive than usual to make decisions based on legitimate business criteria.

In any downsizing, however, it is a good idea to review the demographics of the employees scheduled for termination prior to making final decisions. If the downsizing disproportionately affects a protected category of employees, the company may be leaving itself open to a claim of disparate impact discrimination. The disproportionate effect of the company's selection process could even suggest intentional discrimination, that is, that the company purposefully considered a forbidden criterion.

Finally, the federal Worker Adjustment and Retraining Act, known as the WARN Act, requires medium-sized and large employers to comply with notification requirements when terminating significant numbers of employees. WARN applies to employers who have at least a hundred full-time employees or a hundred employees who together work at least four thousand hours a week, excluding overtime. If an employer subject to WARN either lays off or terminates at least a third of the employees at a site, and that action affects fifty or more employees, or shuts down a site resulting in the layoff or termination of at least fifty employees, then the employer most provide at least sixty days' advance warning to the affected employees. The employer must also notify specified state or local officials and comply with any relevant state or local laws regarding mass downsizings and termination payments.

To summarize, the concepts of employment-at-will and its exceptions, which I have discussed throughout this book, are the basic building blocks you should use when considering whether it would be legal to terminate an employee. The exceptions can be complex and heavily dependent on specific facts, and they vary on a state-by-state basis. The analysis can be further complicated by specialized legislation such as the WARN Act, which applies to large-scale downsizings, and by specific state statutes. Even given the complexities, however, you should have a good sense of the foundational legal principles that apply to employee terminations. In the next three sections, I discuss specialized applications of these principles.

■ Misuse of E-Mail and the Internet

I regularly survey my executive education classes to see how many managers work at companies that have fired employees for misuse of e-mail or the Internet. Typically between a third

and half of the managers respond affirmatively. These percent-
ages should not be a surprise if you have followed media reports
on this topic. During the past few years Hewlett-Packard, Dow
Chemical, Pillsbury, EdwardJones, and many other companies
have fired employees on these grounds. In this section, I discuss
why companies take these issues so seriously and their legal
rights and obligations in this area.

■ Fact or Fallacy? ■

1. Henry, an employee of an investment banking
   firm, recently received what he thought was a
   humorous message making fun of ebonics. He
   forwarded it to some friends within the company.
   African American employees sued the firm,
   alleging that the e-mail created a racially hostile
   environment. The firm is liable.   □ Fact   □ Fallacy

2. To encourage employees to use the company
   e-mail system, Pillsbury announced that it would
   treat e-mail as confidential. Later an employee
   used the e-mail system to send offensive comments to his supervisor. Pillsbury may legally fire
   the employee for inappropriate use of the e-mail
   system.   □ Fact   □ Fallacy

3. A former employee of Intel began sending e-mail
   to current Intel employees arguing that the
   company discriminates against employees and
   otherwise treats them poorly. Intel can successfully order the former employee to stop using
   Intel's e-mail system to communicate with
   current employees.   □ Fact   □ Fallacy

Concerns with Productivity

One area of concern about inappropriate e-mail and Internet use
has to do with legitimate worries about employee productivity.
An employee who spends hours each day in Internet chat rooms
with distant friends is not likely to be meeting an employer's legitimate productivity expectations. As a result, some employers

forbid any personal use of the company's e-mail and Internet system. Other companies permit reasonable personal use of e-mail and Internet systems, believing that productivity will not be harmed and might even be enhanced if employees can accomplish necessary personal tasks through the technology instead of having to leave work.

Deciding what is appropriate at your company is largely a management prerogative. Other than the labor law issues I discuss in the next part, laws impose few constraints on your choice. To avoid allegations that the policy is discriminatory, however, either it should be applied uniformly to all employees or any distinctions should be carefully drawn so as to avoid being based on illegal criteria.

Concerns with Legal Liability

In addition to productivity concerns, employers take misuse of e-mail and the Internet seriously because that misuse can create legal liability for employers. For example, African American employees sued Morgan Stanley for $30 million, arguing that racist jokes circulated via e-mail created an illegal hostile environment at the firm. That case serves as the basis for the Fact or Fallacy? item 1. Morgan Stanley was successful in getting the suit dismissed prior to trial because the plaintiffs had not suffered any negative employment consequences and the e-mail was not targeted at the plaintiffs.[7] A similar lawsuit against Citibank met with the same result—a decision for Citibank.[8] Other companies, however, have not been so fortunate. A suit filed by female employees at Chevron alleged that e-mail messages circulated at the company constituted sexual harassment, and Chevron settled for $2.2 million.[9]

Consider the principles of hostile environment discrimination law that I discussed in Chapter Three. If posting lewd photographs, telling jokes with sexual content, and other like conduct can constitute an illegal hostile environment, then it should not surprise you that the same content transmitted in electronic form could violate the law. Your obligation as a manager to monitor and prohibit such conduct among your employees is just as important when the lewd picture is used as a screen saver as when it hangs above an employee's desk. Both actions have similar effects on the workplace.

Concerns with Insubordination

In some cases, employers decide to terminate employees who have used e-mail to communicate messages that are insubordinate. One example that shows the flexibility management has in these situations occurred at Pillsbury and serves as the basis for Fact or Fallacy? item 2. Because the company wanted to encourage internal e-mail use, Pillsbury "repeatedly assured its employees . . . that all e-mail communications would remain confidential and privileged. . . . [Pillsbury] further assured its employees . . . that e-mail communications could not be intercepted and used by [Pillsbury] against its employees as grounds for termination or reprimand."[10] Following these assurances, an employee, Michael Smyth, exchanged what Pillsbury decided were inappropriate e-mail messages with his supervisor. As an example, the court stated that the e-mail reportedly "concerned sales management and contained threats to 'kill the backstabbing bastards' and referred to the planned holiday party as the 'Jim Jones Koolaid affair.'"[11] As a result, Pillsbury fired Smyth.

Smyth sued Pillsbury, alleging that the firing violated public policy in Pennsylvania because Pillsbury violated his right to privacy. Pillsbury argued that Smyth was an at-will employee and, moreover, that he did not have a reasonable expectation of privacy when voluntarily communicating with his manager over the company e-mail system. In essence, the company argued, Smyth gave up any right of privacy that Pillsbury's former statements promised him when he sent the e-mail in question to his boss, a member of Pillsbury management. The court agreed with Pillsbury and dismissed Smyth's suit before trial.

As a general matter, other courts have agreed with the Pillsbury court and permitted employers to fire employees for inappropriate e-mail use. In the next subsection, however, I will discuss protections for employees who are engaging in concerted activities and how those protections apply to e-mail use.

Courts have consistently upheld the right of employers to monitor employee e-mail. As I write this book, only one state, Connecticut, even requires employers to notify employees of e-mail monitoring. Some attorneys have speculated that federal wiretapping laws may limit employer monitoring of e-mail, but there appears to be little in the way of relevant case law on that point. Of course, if an employer's goal in monitoring e-mail use is to discourage inappropriate use, whatever the employer's policies define that to be, then it seems sensible to notify employees of the monitoring. Employees who know their e-mail is monitored may be less likely to violate company policies than are employees left unaware of the monitoring.

Concerns with Former Employees

The last Fact or Fallacy? item is based on an actual incident at Intel. Intel fired Kourosh Kenneth Hamidi after years of disputes over Hamidi's workers' compensation claims. Hamidi believed Intel illegally fired him because of his age. To get attention for his grievances against the company, Hamidi took a variety of actions, including sending critical e-mail messages to thousands of Intel employees and handing out copies of the e-mail while dressed as a cowboy and riding a horse. Intel went to court, asking for an order prohibiting Hamidi from continuing to send e-mail to its employees via the company's computer system. Intel claims that Hamidi's e-mail campaign is a form of trespass on company property. Hamidi argues the e-mail messages are protected free speech.[12] Intel has won so far in court,[13] but the case is now before the California Supreme Court. That court's decision will determine the scope of a former employee's rights in California and may be influential in future cases in other states as well.[14]

The bottom line is that the legal principles in this area are developing as technology changes. In some instances it is quite easy to analyze a situation under traditional legal standards. In others, the traditional principles do not fit very well. As a result, you and sometimes your lawyer will need to make judgment calls on how the legal system will treat a new and novel question. That may cause you some discomfort, however, it is little different from other facets of your job where you need to take business risks with new technologies, changing markets, and so forth.

■ Concerted Activities

Most managers know that federal laws protect employees' rights to unionize. Once employees form a union, laws require employers to bargain in good faith, limit the permanent replacement of striking employees, and provide other rights to union members. In this section, I will discuss a few of the labor law concepts that apply to employee terminations.

■ Fact or Fallacy? ■

---

1. Complexities Corporation is a small, nonunionized company. Dora, a manager at Complexities, recently hired Karl, who is suggesting to other employees that they form a union. Despite the principle of employment-at-will, it is illegal for Dora to fire Karl in order to stop the unionizing effort.   ☐ Fact   ☐ Fallacy

■ **Fact or Fallacy?, Cont'd** ■

2. Mega Manufacturing recently caught Joanne, a
   member of the union at Mega, stealing a roll of
   masking tape. Because of the theft, Mega can fire
   Joanne without regard for her status as a union
   member.   ☐ Fact   ☐ Fallacy

3. Leinweber, an employee at a small nonunion
   company, recently sent an e-mail message to
   the COO and all other employees criticizing the
   company's new vacation policy and suggesting
   that other employees complain about the policy.
   The employment-at-will doctrine permits the
   company to fire Leinweber.   ☐ Fact   ☐ Fallacy

Organizing Activities

Technically, federal labor law governs the actions of employees,
employers, and union organizers. Labor law is far too vast and
complex a field for me to address thoroughly in this book. One key
provision, however, states, "Employees shall have the right to self-
organization, to form, join, or assist labor organizations, . . . and to
engage in other concerted activities for the purpose of . . . mutual
aid or protection. . . ."[15]

This language provides significant protections to employees during a union organizing effort. For a nonunion employer,
an organizing effort can cause great concern. The employer may
not have experience in dealing with a unionized workforce, may
be apprehensive about the collective bargaining process, may be
concerned about the potential effect on its labor costs, and may
even worry about the implications for the morale of employees
who do not wish to be part of a union.

Whatever the reasons, many employers confronted with
a union organizing effort want to discourage it. This is almost
always a situation where the employer should obtain ongoing

advice from an attorney experienced in dealing with unionizing campaigns. Even well-intentioned attempts to influence employees can easily run afoul of the law. The law does permit employers to communicate their views about unionizing efforts. For example, an employer may remind employees of the workplace benefits they currently enjoy and may compare those benefits to those offered by competitors. However, the law also limits employer communications. For example, an employer cannot promise future benefit enhancements or pay raises if the employees choose not to unionize. It can be very difficult for someone who is not experienced in the intricacies of this area to determine which specific communications are permitted. And an error can have serious consequences. In some cases it may even permit union advocates to seek a second vote.

The law clearly prohibits employers from firing employees for unionizing activities or for supporting a union. Similarly, an employer cannot threaten to fire, demote, take away pay or benefits, or otherwise take negative action against an employee who is active in unionizing efforts, or who supports a union, because of those activities. While the importance of these laws in protecting employees' rights to unionize is clear, the limitations also create issues for employers who wish to terminate employees for legitimate reasons, not relating to the union, during an organizing campaign. The employer may later be forced to explain the reasons for the termination and to provide evidence that the real reason did not have anything to do with the unionization effort. Certainly, in the case described in the first Fact or Fallacy item, Dora cannot fire Karl because he advocates forming a union.

Terminating a Unionized Employee

I noted in Chapter One that in managing unionized workforces the doctrine of employment-at-will has very limited, if any, application. That is because management is required by law to engage in good faith bargaining on topics such as wages, benefits, hours, and other terms and conditions of employment. Once the company enters into a collective bargaining agreement with the union representatives and the relevant employees approve the agreement, then the terms of the employer-employee relationship are largely governed by that agreement. Many agreements permit management to terminate employees only for specific reasons such as good cause, provide for seniority rights in downsizings and job selection, and so forth.

Furthermore, most collective bargaining agreements contain procedures for management and employees to follow in resolving disputes. Typically, employee complaints must be filed initially as grievances, which are negotiated with management by union representatives. Outside arbitrators may be used if none of the internal processes are successful in settling the problem, but court action may be limited. Frequently these types of provisions govern cases where individuals dispute the termination of their employment. So, prior to terminating a unionized employee, it is important at most companies to discuss the situation with representatives from the company's union relations staff. Doing so helps ensure that the proper procedures are followed and that documentation is maintained. Even in cases of employee malfeasance, such as outlined in Fact or Fallacy item 2, the union retains an obligation to represent the employee.

Labor Law in Nonunionized Workplaces

Federal labor laws that provide employees with the right to unionize also protect nonunionized employees who would be entitled to form a union but who have no interest in joining a union. These laws even apply when no unionizing campaign is under way. This is one of the aspects of employment law that most surprises managers in executive education programs I teach. Most managers initially think this provision of the law is irrational.

Why should laws about unionization apply to employees who are not even considering forming or joining a union?

The basic answer is in the statutory language that I quoted in the discussion of organizing activities. That language protects the right of employees to "engage in other concerted activities." The courts and the National Labor Relations Board (NLRB), which also hears cases dealing with the federal labor laws, have defined concerted activities broadly. The Supreme Court has stated that the term "embraces the activities of employees who have joined together in order to achieve common goals."[16] Even one nonmanagerial employee who speaks out can be engaging in concerted activities. The Board has said that "concerted activity may consist solely of a speaker and a listener, so long as the speaker is seeking to induce group action."[17] And, remember, the import of the statute is that an employer cannot terminate, threaten, or take any other negative action against an employee for engaging in concerted activities.

To tie this discussion in with the earlier consideration of e-mail and Internet use, consider Timekeeping System's termination of Lawrence Leinweber. A simplified version of this case forms the basis for the third Fact or Fallacy? item. Barry Markwitz, the COO of Timekeeping Systems, sent a message to all twenty-three or so employees about a change in vacation policy. Markwitz's message explained that the new policy would be more favorable to employees under some circumstances and asked for comments. Leinweber e-mailed a response to Markwitz pointing out a minor error in the calculations. Markwitz did not respond, but another employee sent a supportive message about the policy to a group of coworkers, including Leinweber. Leinweber then sent a long message to all employees objecting to the new policy. The NLRB characterized that message as containing some "flippant and rather grating language."[18]

In response to Leinweber's second e-mail message, Markwitz wrote a memo to him stating that Leinweber had violated the company's policy requiring courtesy and respect in the work-place. He said that he would terminate Leinweber unless Lein-weber sent another e-mail explaining the inappropriate nature of his second message. The two had numerous conversations on the topic but could not come to agreement. After Leinweber failed to write the requested e-mail, Markwitz fired him.

Leinweber then filed suit, claiming that his termination vi-olated the labor laws' protections for concerted activity. The NLRB agreed that Leinweber's e-mail message to his fellow em-ployees was intended to seek support for the common goal of opposing the new vacation policy. Moreover, the Board was con-vinced that part of the reason Markwitz was so offended by the e-mail was its broad distribution to other employees—in short, its "concerted" nature.

The final question the NLRB addressed in the case was whether the flippant and grating tone of the e-mail voided the protection Leinweber otherwise was entitled to under federal law. There is an exception from protection for language that is "so violent or of such serious character as to render the em-ployee unfit for further service."[19] That exception is important because it permits employers to fire employees for grossly in-subordinate or violent acts even if those acts are undertaken in order to seek support from fellow employees on changes in em-ployer policy. The NLRB, however, did not believe that Leinwe-ber's language crossed the threshold of being so serious as to void his legal rights.

While this case might strike you as being one that you can-not envision occurring at your company—perhaps because your company is much larger, because it would be unusual to solicit the comments of all employees about a change in benefits pol-icy, or for some other reason—it is important to consider it from a broader perspective. Numerous cases confirm the right of nonunion employees to seek the support of their coworkers in challenging company policies or discussing employment issues with management. Increasing numbers of the cases seem to be situations where employees have employed technology to broaden their communication efforts.

When an employee seems to be stirring up fellow workers against some company action or policy, it often feels natural for a manager to view the employee as a troublemaker and take some type of action. If this happens in your workforce, I suggest that you review the situation with a lawyer to ensure you do not impinge on the employee's right to engage in concerted activities. The penalties can be significant. Timekeeping Systems was required to reinstate Leinweber, to make him whole for any lost earnings and benefits, and to post at all of its facilities a notice approved by the NLRB that outlined employees' rights to concerted activity and explained the company's obligation to reinstate and pay Leinweber.[20]

To sum up, the federal labor laws apply to situations where employees are attempting to unionize, to workforces that are already unionized, and to nonunion employees who have no interest in joining a union but who want to work together or seek support from fellow employees in changing the terms, conditions, or privileges of their employment. The federal labor laws prohibit you from terminating an employee for, among other reasons, engaging in permitted unionizing efforts or in concerted activities more generally. Because of the specialized nature of these situations and the complexity of the relevant law, I suggest you seek legal counsel if faced with challenges of this nature in your workplace.

■ Employer Liability for Employees Who Harm Nonemployees

Legal standards encourage you as a manager to treat it as a serious problem if you have an employee who poses a risk of harm to nonemployees. The situation could result in liability to your company. And the only way to avoid that liability may be to terminate the employee before any harm occurs.

■ Fact or Fallacy? ■

---

1. A pizza company takes extraordinary care to hire good drivers and train them to drive carefully when they are delivering pizza. Yet if a careless employee runs a stoplight and kills a pedestrian, the company is still liable.   ☐ Fact   ☐ Fallacy

2. Henry, a truck driver at Large Truck Co., lost his temper with the driver of a truck Henry was following while on the job. When the two vehicles stopped at a light, Henry dragged the driver out of his cab and stabbed him in the leg. Since this occurred during Henry's working hours, Large Truck Co. is liable for Henry's actions.   ☐ Fact   ☐ Fallacy

3. Jane Wagner, a lawyer who had billed 307 hours the prior month, was making business calls on her cell phone while she drove home from a late meeting with a client. She inadvertently swerved her Mercedes and killed fifteen-year-old Naeun Yoon. Wagner pleaded guilty. The law firm that employed Wagner is liable for Yoon's death.   ☐ Fact   ☐ Fallacy

---

Managers are often shocked to learn that employers typically are responsible for injuries caused by an employee who is careless on the job. This is true even if the company has taken all possible actions to train, instruct, and supervise the employee in safe ways of performing the job.

The legal concept at work here is known as vicarious liability, or *respondeat superior*. The general rule is that an employer is liable for all acts of an employee undertaken within the scope of employment. A four-part test exists to determine whether an employee is within the scope of employment. First, is the conduct of the kind the person was employed to perform? Second, did the conduct occur substantially within authorized time and space limits? Third, is the conduct actuated at least in part by a purpose to serve the employer? Fourth, if the employee intentionally used force against another person, was the force not unexpected by the employer?[21]

As a hypothetical example, consider the case of a pizza company that offers home delivery (Fact or Fallacy? item 1). The company takes all possible measures to ensure that its employees drive with extreme care while delivering pizza. This could include periodic checks of employee driving records, regular training to remind employees of driving safety, modifications to the delivery cars to limit maximum speed, and so forth. But, if, while making a scheduled delivery, a careless employee runs a stop sign and kills a pedestrian, the company is likely to be liable because the four-part test almost certainly shows that the driver was acting in the scope of employment. This may seem harsh and unfair to an employer who has gone to great lengths to ensure its employees drive safely. But this legal principle provides a strong incentive for employers to monitor employee behavior. Only by preventing injury to others can the employer avoid liability.

On the other hand, the test for scope of employment permits employers to avoid liability when employees deviate significantly from their assigned jobs or take totally unexpected actions. For example, consider the situation outlined in Fact or Fallacy? item 2. In the actual case, Oscar Gonzalez was driving a tractor-trailer rig for his employer, Land Transport. Gonzalez repeatedly attempted to pass Robert Nichols, another truck driver. Nichols responded with obscene gestures, and Gonzalez started tailgating Nichols. Eventually both trucks stopped at a traffic light, where both Gonzalez and Nichols got out of their trucks. Nichols then attacked Gonzalez with a cable. Gonzalez pulled out a knife and stabbed Nichols.

Nichols sued Land Transport, alleging that it was liable for his injuries since Gonzalez was acting within the scope of his employment. The court applied the test I just outlined. One of the requirements is that the employee's actions must be taken at least in part to serve the employer. The court noted that "actions that are done with a private, rather than a work-related, purpose to commit wrongdoing are outside of the scope of employment. . . ."[22] Also, the court believed that when Gonzalez exited from the truck cab, he left the physical space where Land Transport expected him to work. Finally, Gonzalez's crime was a serious one and was not similar in nature to actions expected by Land Transport.[23] Therefore, Land Transport was not liable for the injuries Gonzalez inflicted on Nichols.

To close this section, consider the facts summarized in the final Fact or Fallacy? item. The law firm of Cooley Godward viewed Jane Wagner as a hardworking and well-regarded attorney before she swerved her car and killed Naeun Yoon while doing business on her cell phone. Wagner continued driving, believing that she had hit a deer. She turned herself in when she heard on the news the next morning that a fifteen-year-old had been killed by a hit-and-run driver. Wagner pleaded guilty and was sentenced to jail. Yoon's heirs sued Cooley Godward for $30 million, alleging that Wagner was acting within the scope of her employment when she killed Yoon.[24] The case has not yet been decided, but the judge has ruled that it is strong enough to go forward.[25]

Taken together, the material on an employer's liability for acts of employees within the scope of employment should make you more aware of the importance of developing appropriate policies and managerial approaches to prevent your employees from causing harm to others. For example, numerous companies have responded to the cases involving injuries incurred as a result of an employee's driving while talking on a cell phone—the Wagner case is not the only one of its kind—by developing policies against cell phone use while driving. Remember, though, those policies do not preclude employer liability if an employee disobeys the policy. So you, as a manager, need to ensure that your employees walk the talk—that they act in accordance with company policies. Although it may seem harsh, you should consider terminating any employee who does not comply because the principle of respondeat superior means the company will be liable for harm that individual causes to nonemployees while acting in the scope of employment.

■ Process Considerations in Terminating an Employee

Managers often ask me about the proper procedures to use when terminating an employee. Are employees entitled to a warning? Must warnings be in writing? Should an employee have the opportunity to resign rather than being fired? Who should be the one to tell an employee about being fired?

The bottom line is that the legal system imposes relatively few constraints on the procedure you use to terminate an employee. Other than laws like the WARN Act, which requires employers making large-scale downsizings to give advance notice to employees, there is no generalized legal requirement that you give an employee advance notice of termination. Similarly, no law that I know of requires you to warn an employee whose behavior or performance is unacceptable. Instead, these tend to be business decisions and can be made according to the circumstances at hand. For example, if economic conditions force you to lay off employees but the company can afford to give them two weeks' notice, then that may be a humane approach. Giving notice may improve morale among the employees who remain and make the company more attractive to job candidates if it rebounds and begins hiring. On the other hand, some companies have concerns with technology transfer or trade secrets and decide to terminate employment immediately upon giving notice.

The general flexibility accorded to managers when terminating employees does not mean, however, that you do not have to worry about any legal standards. For example, most states establish by law a maximum time period for you to provide the employee with the final paycheck. Some even require that an employee who is fired receive that paycheck immediately upon termination. State and federal laws also address benefits, frequently permitting employees to continue their company-sponsored health insurance for some period of time or giving them the right to convert the insurance to an individual policy.

Who tells an employee of the termination, whether the employee is given an official letter regarding the termination, and whether the company asks the employee to release legal claims against the company in return for a severance package all tend to be business decisions, though the legal system regulates the enforceability of waivers. If your company uses written documentation that goes to a terminated employee, it is important to have it reviewed by an attorney who is knowledgeable about employment law issues. As I discussed earlier in this book, there may be situations where it is an appropriate business decision to give an employee an opportunity to resign or to offer a positive letter of recommendation in return for a resignation. The law does not forbid you to make those offers, but, as I have discussed, you should be mindful of the risk of negative legal ramifications.

Practically speaking, regardless of the reason you have for terminating an employee, it is good practice to treat a departing employee professionally and humanely. Studies indicate that former employees who think they were treated unfairly or inappropriately are more likely to sue because of their termination than individuals who, though they may be unhappy about losing their jobs, feel that they were treated with consideration. The termination and how it is carried out may also affect the remaining workforce. Especially if the terminated employee has friends who will continue working at the company, it will probably benefit morale and productivity, as well as your own reputation as a reasonable manager, if you treat the departing employee with respect.

■ Conclusion

By way of summing up this chapter's discussion, let's reconsider the issues facing Richard in the opening scenario. Abcure's vice president in charge of benefits is insisting that Donna be fired because of an e-mail message Donna sent to all division employees objecting to the new health insurance program. Assuming that Donna is an employee-at-will, it seems at first glance that Abcure can fire her if it wants to. This situation, however, should remind you of the case lost by Timekeeping Systems. Even though Donna is not a unionized employee, as a nonmanagement employee she has the legal right to engage in concerted activity in the workplace. Because she sent the e-mail to fellow employees to encourage them to seek rescission of the new policy, it appears that Donna was engaging in a protected concerted activity. Donna's e-mail, however, was vitriolic. Because the law permits employers to terminate employees whose actions are so egregious that the employee is unfit for future service, Richard may want to review the e-mail with an attorney to determine if it meets that standard.

Kolbe's complaint about Jergen's calling him to look at pornographic Web sites raises another set of problems for Richard. If Jergen's conduct is severe or pervasive enough to rise to the level of hostile environment, Abcure could face liability if Richard fails to investigate the complaint and take reasonable and speedy action to resolve the situation. However, this situation is complicated by the fact that the two employees are the same gender. While that does not preclude a hostile environment claim, it does makes such a claim potentially problematic. Furthermore, it is unclear whether Kolbe has experienced any tangible job detriment. Nevertheless, Richard should be aware that employees' use of technology can result in potential liability for Abcure for harassment or discrimination.

The final problem Richard faces is with Stewart, a high-performing employee who appears to be an unsafe driver. Because Stewart's job as a field representative requires him to drive as part of his job, Abcure faces the possibility of legal liability. If Stewart injures someone while acting in the course of his employment, then the concept of respondeat superior probably will mean that Abcure has liability for the injury. Richard may decide that the risk is too great and that he should terminate Stewart to avoid future problems. Alternatively, Richard and the human resources representative may decide to give Stewart another chance but counsel him on the need to be more careful, at least while engaged in company business. They should, however, understand that Abcure may be liable regardless of the steps they take to ensure that employees drive safely.

CHAPTER SUMMARY

The chapter reminds managers that employment-at-will is the foundation concept that governs employee terminations. Employment-at-will is limited by the exceptions of contract and public policy, as well as by detailed legal regulation such as the nondiscrimination laws discussed in Chapters Four and Five. Both the contract and public policy exceptions, however, tend to be interpreted narrowly by the courts.

The increasing availability of technology in the workplace has prompted managers to become concerned about the effect of that technology on productivity, workplace hostile environment legal claims, and insubordination. In most cases companies have won legal challenges to their right to fire employees for violating company policy on Internet and e-mail use. The one exception occurs where a nonmanagement employee uses e-mail or the Internet to communicate with fellow employees about issues such as pay and benefits.

The chapter closed with brief discussions of unionizing efforts, unionized workplaces, and nonunionized employees who engage in concerted activity as well as situations where employees may cause harm to nonemployees. Each of these circumstances tends to require managers to carefully consider the implications of terminating an employee.

In sum, this chapter raises and refines many of the concepts discussed throughout this book. The doctrine of employment-at-will grants managers much discretion in hiring, in promoting or demoting, and in firing employees. But numerous legal constructs, at federal, state, and local levels, act to constrain managerial actions. My overarching goal in this book has been to introduce you to some of the basic legal concepts that are important as you manage your workforce on a day-to-day basis so that you will be more comfortable in approaching employment law issues as business decisions. As when you encounter other business decisions with specialized risk factors, it may be critical that you consult an attorney who is knowledgeable about employment cases to assist you in analyzing the risk posed by various approaches. You should feel confident, though, that you understand many of the basic building blocks that the attorney will rely on in analyzing the situation so that you can be an informed client.

Ultimately, no attorney can guarantee that a job candidate, employee, or former employee will not sue over a negative action you take. But this is no different from the other business decisions you face. As a manager you deal with risk on a daily basis. In employment matters, as in all your other areas of responsibility, your success depends on your ability and willingness to weigh the risks and benefits of potential actions. I hope the basic legal principles you have learned in this book will make you more confident in managing risk when it comes to the decisions you make with regard to your employees, and more aware of when you should seek expert counsel.

Notes

Chapter One

1. "Retired Wide Receiver Catches $10M Jury Award," *National Law Journal* (February 7, 2000): A15. A court later reduced the award to $6.1 million. M. Fisk, "Creative Plaintiffs' Counsel Target Employers, Ballparks and Laser-Eye Surgeons, A Survey on Emerging Causes of Action Shows," *New Jersey Law Journal* (December 18, 2000).

2. *Wanamaker v. Columbian Rope Co.,* 907 F. Supp. 522, 538 (N.D.N.Y. 1995).

3. C. Hymowitz, "Using Layoffs to Battle Downturns Often Costs More Than It Saves," *Wall Street Journal* (July 24, 2001): B1.

4. L. Pechman, "Appearance-Based Discrimination," *New York Law Journal* (September 25, 1996).

5. S. Baderian and J. Kozak, "Claims of Retaliation Continue to Increase," *National Law Journal* (November 20, 2000): B13.

6. *Bammert v. Don's SuperValu, Inc.,* 632 N.W.2d 124 (Wis. 2001).

7. *Guz v. Bechtel,* 8 P.3d 1089 (Cal. 2001).

8. *New York v. Wal-Mart,* 207 A.D.2d 150 (N.Y. Sup. Ct. 1995).

9. J. Bravin, "U.S. Courts are Tough on Job-Bias Suits," *Wall Street Journal* (July 16, 2001): A2.

10. A. Longstreth, "Sears Starts an ADR Program for Its Retailers," *National Law Journal* (January 7, 2002): A21.

Chapter Two

1. "Best Practices of Private Sector Employers," *The U.S. Equal Employ-ment Opportunity Commission.* Available on-line: http://www.eeoc.gov/task/practice.html. Access date: December 27, 2002.
2. *King* v. *Trans World Airlines, Inc.,* 738 F.2d 255, 256 (8th Cir., 1984).
3. *Byrnie* v. *Cromwell Board of Education,* 243 F.3d 93, 110 (2d Cir. 2001).
4. *Rummery* v. *Illinois Bell Telephone Co.,* 250 F.3d 553, 558–559 (7th Cir. 2001).
5. C. McGlothen, "Hiring and Legal Risks," *National Law Journal* (April 29, 2002): A28.
6. C. Marquet, "Creating a Comprehensive Violence Prevention Pro-gram," *Connecticut Employment Law Letter* (September 2001).
7. J. Wefing, "Employer Drug Testing: Disparate Judicial and Legislative Responses," *Albany Law Review* 63 (2000): 815, note 147.
8. Greenebaum Doll and McDonald PLLC, "Court Enforces Subpoena for Employer's Preemployment Tests, Validation Studies," *Kentucky Em-ployment Law Letter* (September 2001).
9. "9th Circuit OKs Teacher Skills Test Despite Disparate Impact," *School Law Bulletin* (December 13, 2000).
10. L. Lavelle, "Resumes: Beware of Getting 'Creative,'" *Business Week* (October 22, 2001): 134.
11. "Coaches' Resumes Attract Notice," *USA Today* (February 7, 2002): 14C.
12. P. Page, "Boss Liable for Rape by Driver," *National Law Journal* (Oc-tober 1, 2001): A10.
13. *Yunker* v. *Honeywell Inc.,* 496 N.W.2d 419, 423–24 (Minn. App. 1993).

Chapter Three

1. *Price Waterhouse* v. *Hopkins,* 490 U.S. 228, 235 (1989).
2. Ibid.
3. A. Hopkins, *So Ordered* (Amherst, Mass.: University of Massachu-setts Press, 1996), pp. 25, 51.

4. *Price Waterhouse* v. *Hopkins,* note 1, at 234.

5. Compare *Menchaca* v. *Ottenwalder,* No. 99–55082, 2001 U.S. App. LEXIS 19557, *3 (9th Cir., Aug. 29, 2001), with *Bostic* v. *AT&T,* 166 F. Supp. 2d 350, (D. V.I. 2001) (quoting *Smith* v. *Secretary of Navy,* 659 F.2d 1113, 1120 (D.C. Cir. 1981).

6. *Wilcox* v. *State Farm Mutual Automobile Insurance Company,* 253 F.3d 1069 (8th Cir. 2001).

7. *Vaughn* v. *Texaco,* 918 F.2d 517, 519 (5th Cir. 1990).

8. Ibid. at 523.

9. E. Garsten, "Ford Settles, Admits No Wrong," *Legal Intelligencer* (December 19, 2001): 4.

10. *Ferrett* v. *General Motors Corp.,* 438 Mich. 235 (1991).

11. *Brattis* v. *Rainbow Advertising Holdings, L.L.C.,* No. 99 Civ. 10144 (NRB), 2000 U.S. Dist. LEXIS 7345, at *3 (S.D.N.Y. May 31, 2000).

12. Ibid. at 10.

13. Ibid.

14. M. Cooper, "Job Reference Immunity Statutes: Prevalent but Irrelevant," *Cornell Journal of Law and Public Policy* 11 (Fall 2001): 1–68. See page 3, note 5.

15. *Moore* v. *St. Joseph Nursing Home,* 184 Mich. App. 766 (Mich. Ct. App. 1990).

16. A. Weitzman and others, "Employee's References May Spawn Litigation," *National Law Journal* (May 19, 1997)" B4.

17. *Randi W.* v. *Muroc Joint Unified School District,* 14 Cal. 4th 1066, 1071–1072 (Cal. 1997).

18. Ibid. at 1070.

19. J. Lublin, "Bosses Beware: Michael Rankin is Taking Notes," *Wall Street Journal* (November 14, 1996): B1.

Chapter Four

1. *Bibby* v. *Philadelphia Coca-Cola Bottling Co.,* 260 F.3d 257 (3rd Cir. 2001).

2. Title VII, Equal Employment Opportunities, 42 U.S.C. § 2000e-2(a).

3. *Sanchez* v. *Denver Public Schools,* 164 F.3d 527 (10th Cir. 1998).

4. *Watson* v. *Potter,* No. 01–3808, 2002 U.S. App. LEXIS 8625, at *8 (7th Cir. May 1, 2002).

5. *Davis* v. *Sioux City,* 115 F.3d 1365 (8th Cir. 1997).

6. *De la Cruz* v. *New York City,* 82 F.3d 16 (2nd Cir. 1996).

7. *Hoffman-Dombrowski* v. *Arlington International Racecourse, Inc.,* 254 F.3d 644, 651 (7th Cir. 2001).

8. Ibid. at 649.

9. 42 U.S.C. § 2000e-2(e).

10. Bill Hoffmann, "'Jingle' Is Fine, 'Jiggle' Is Not," *New York Post* (October 11, 2000): 29.

11. *Wilson* v. *Southwest Airlines Co.,* 517 F. Supp. 292, 304 (N.D. Tex. 1981) (citation omitted).

12. *Healey* v. *Southwood Psychiatric Hosp.,* 78 F.3d 128 (3d Cir. 1996).

13. *E.E.O.C.* v. *Hi 40 Corp.,* 953 F. Supp. 301 (W. Mo. 1996).

14. *Meritor Savings Bank* v. *Vinson,* 477 U.S. 57 (1986).

15. Ibid.

16. *Harris* v. *Forklift Sys.,* 510 U.S. 17, 23 (1993).

17. *Hurston* v. *Henderson,* No. 260–98–7055X, 2001 EEOPUB LEXIS 366, *5–6 (January 19, 2001).

18. "Terminating Employee for Violating Company Policy Upheld by Boise Judge," *Utah Employment Law Letter* (August 2001).

Chapter Five

1. *Sutton* v. *United Airlines, Inc.,* 119 S. Ct. 2139 (1999).

2. *Toyota Motor Manufacturing* v. *Williams,* 122 S. Ct. 681 (2002).

3. 29 C.F.R. § 1630.2(h)(2).

4. *EEOC Technical Assistance Manual,* § 2.3(a) (1992).

5. *U.S. Airways Inc.* v. *Barnett,* 535 U.S. 391 (2002).

6. *EEOC* v. *United Parcel Service, Inc.,* 249 F.3d 557, 560 (6th Cir. 2001).

7. Ibid. at 563 (quoting *Burns* v. *Coca-Cola Enterprises,* 222 F.3d 247, 257 (6th Cir. 2000).

8. 42 U.S.C. § 12113(b).

9. *Palmer* v. *Circuit Court of Cook County,* Ill., 117 F.3d 351 (1997).

10. *EEOC Technical Assistance Manual,* § 4.5 (1992).

11. 42 U.S.C. § 12113(b).

12. *Chevron U.S.A. Inc.* v. *Echazabal,* 536 U.S. 73 (2002).

13. 42 U.S.C. § 12114(a).

14. 42 U.S.C. § 12114(c)(1).

15. 42 U.S.C. § 12114(c)(4).

16. *Allison* v. *Pepsi-Cola Bottling Co.,* 183 Mich. App. 101, 109 (Mich. App. 1990).

17. Ibid. at 112.

Chapter Six

1. Denlinger, Rothenthal, and Greenberg, "Discussion of Future Plans Not a Promise of Continued Employment," *Ohio Employment Law Letter* 13 (April 2002).

2. Denlinger, Rothenthal, and Greenberg, "Discussion of Future Plans Not a Promise . . . "

3. *Redricks* v. *Industrial Vehicles Intl., Inc.,* 2002 OK 13 (2002).

4. Ibid.

5. *Rowan* v. *Tractor Supply Co.,* 263 Va. 209, 211 (2002).

6. Ibid. at 215.

7. "Judge Throws Out Bias Suit Filed Against Morgan Stanley," *Newsday* (July 19, 1997): A27.

8. *Curtis* v. *DiMaio,* No. 99–7468, 2000 U.S. App. LEXIS 902 (2nd Cir. Jan. 25, 2000).

9. Kyung M. Song, "Personal Use of Workplace E-Mail Is a Gray Area at Many Companies," *St. Louis Post-Dispatch* (May 9, 1999): E1.

10. *Smyth* v. *The Pillsbury Co.,* 914 F. Supp. 97, 98 (E.D. Penn. 1996).

11. Ibid.

12. Allyce Bess, "E-Mail Crusade Against Intel: Is It Trespass?" *Wall Street Journal* (August 14, 2002): B1.

13. *Intel Corp.* v. *Hamidi,* 94 Cal. App. 4th 325 (2001).

14. Bess, "E-Mail Crusade Against Intel."

15. National Labor Relations Act, § 7 (1994).

16. *NLRB* v. *City Disposal Systems Inc.,* 465 U.S. 822 (1984).

17. *Blue Chip Casino* v. *McMillin,* No. 25-CA-27856–1 2002 NLRB LEXIS 383 (Aug. 16, 2002).

18. *Timekeeping Systems, Inc.,* 323 N.L.R.B. 244, 246 (1997).
19. Ibid. at 248.
20. Ibid. at 245.
21. This four-part test is loosely rephrased from § 228 of *Restatement (Second) of Agency* (St. Paul, Minn.: American Law Institute, 1958).
22. *Nichols* v. *Land Transport Corp.,* 103 F. Supp. 2d 25, 27 (D. ME 1999).
23. Ibid. at 27–28.
24. Sara Silver, "Targeting Workers Who Talk and Drive," *Los Angeles Times* (August 27, 2001): C3; Sue Shellenbarger, "Should Employers Play a Role in Safe Use of Cellphones in Cars?" *Wall Street Journal* (July 18, 2001): B1.
25. Arlo Wagner, "Driver's Firm Sued in Death Linked to Phone Use," *Washington Times* (October 27, 2001): A8.

The Author

Dana M. Muir is an associate professor at the University of Michigan Business School, where she also teaches in programs at the Executive Education Center. She has taught at the University of Michigan and University of Iowa law schools. Prior to joining the Business School, Professor Muir practiced law at national law firms based in Chicago and Detroit. She also held a number of human resources positions at Chrysler Corporation.

Professor Muir specializes in employment issues. She has published numerous articles in law reviews, legal journals, and conference proceedings. Her research has been cited by the U.S. Supreme Court. She currently serves as a member of the Department of Labor's Advisory Council on Employee Welfare and Pension Plans. Professor Muir holds a J.D. from the University of Michigan Law School and an M.B.A. from the University of Detroit–Mercy.

Index

65; arbitration as alternative to, 23–25; defamation claims, 70–72, 74–76; defending against discrimination, 91–100; disability claims and, 121–122, 122–124, 125, 128–130, 133–134; employee e-mail/Internet misuse, 157–160; gender discrimination, 11, 34–35, 39, 60–61; negligent claims, 69–70; negligent hiring, 46–47; performance appraisals and, 64–68; privacy rights and, 42–43; racial discrimination, 66–67; recognized as business risk, 25–28; references for former employee and, 74–80; regarding arrest/conviction information, 46–47, 50–51; religious beliefs and harassment, 113; retaliation, 11; termination, 150–154, 157–158, 164–165; transferred employees, 89–90; vicarious liability (*respondeat superior*), 167–170; work-related injuries and, 140–141. *See also* Employment law

Lee, C., 83–84, 91, 108

Legal statutes. *See* Employment law

Leinweber, L., 164

Liability. *See* Employer liability

Libel, 70

"Like Me" syndrome, 33

Lost work time Fact or Fallacy?: FMLA leave and, 136–139; questions listed, 135–136; work-related injuries, 139

M

McConkey, P., 7, 21, 53

McDonnell Douglas approach, 98–99

Maintenance Management Corporation, 75

Managers: avoidance of court system by, 23–25; challenges of employment law for, 1–3; importance of understanding/avoiding discrimination, 83–85;

interviewing candidates, 34–40; issues of lost work time due to disabilities for, 117–119; legal environment facing, 30; legal issues of providing references, 74–80; liability for harassment, 105, 107–111; "Like Me" syndrome of, 33; recognizing employment law issues as business risk, 25–28. *See also* Employers; Evaluating employees

Markwitz, B., 164–165

Mass terminations, 154–155

Medical testing, 41, 42

Mental illness: ADA on threats to others and, 131–132; workplace violence and, 46–47, 78–79

Miller, N., 50

Misuse of e-mail/Internet: concerns with former employees and, 159–160; concerns with insubordination and, 158–159; concerns with legal liability and, 157–158; concerns with productivity and, 156–157; growing trend in employee, 155–156

Misuse of e-mail/Internet Fact or Fallacy?: concerns with former employees, 159–160; concerns with insubordination and, 158–159; employer liability over employee, 157; questions listed, 156

Moore, C. A., Sr., 75

Morgan Stanley, 157

Moulin Rouge (film), 93–94

Mueller, J., 150–151

N

Negligence: hiring employees and, 46–47; hostile environment and employer, 110; performance appraisals and claims of, 69–70

Nesser, K., 50–51

Nichols, R., 168, 169

NLRB (National Labor Relations Board), 164, 165